Cubbon Park

Cubbon Park

The Green Heart of Bengaluru

ROOPA PAI

SPEAKING
TIGER

SPEAKING TIGER BOOKS LLP
125A, Ground Floor, Shahpur Jat, near Asiad Village,
New Delhi 110049

Published by Speaking Tiger Books in hardback 2022

Copyright © Roopa Pai 2022

ISBN: 978-93-5447-218-3
eISBN: 978-93-5447-226-8

10 9 8 7 6 5 4 3 2 1

Typeset in Cardo by SÜRYA, New Delhi
Printed at SBM Industries Pvt. Ltd. Rai

All rights reserved.
No part of this publication may be reproduced, transmitted, or stored in a retrieval system, in any form or by any means, electronic, mechanical, photocopying, recording or otherwise, without the prior permission of the publisher.

This book is sold subject to the condition that it shall not, by way of trade or otherwise, be lent, resold, hired out, or otherwise circulated, without the publisher's prior consent, in any form of binding or cover other than that in which it is published.

Contents

Cubbon Park: Bangalore Central	1
The Making of the People's Park	8

People of the Park: The First 100 Years

The Birthers	25
The Watchers	44
The Enrichers	66

People of the Park: The Last Fifty Years

The Lovers	87
The Guardians	123
The Warriors	132

Epilogue

A Park for the Ages	165
My Cubbon Park	171
Selected Bibliography	175

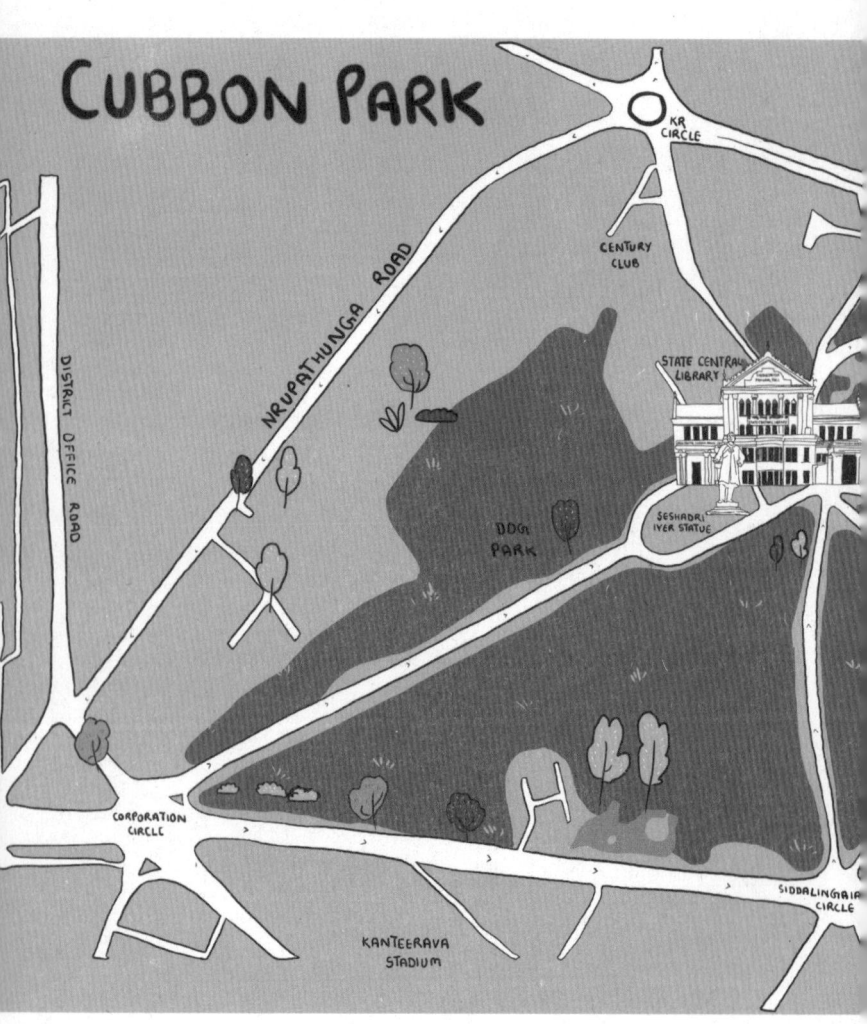

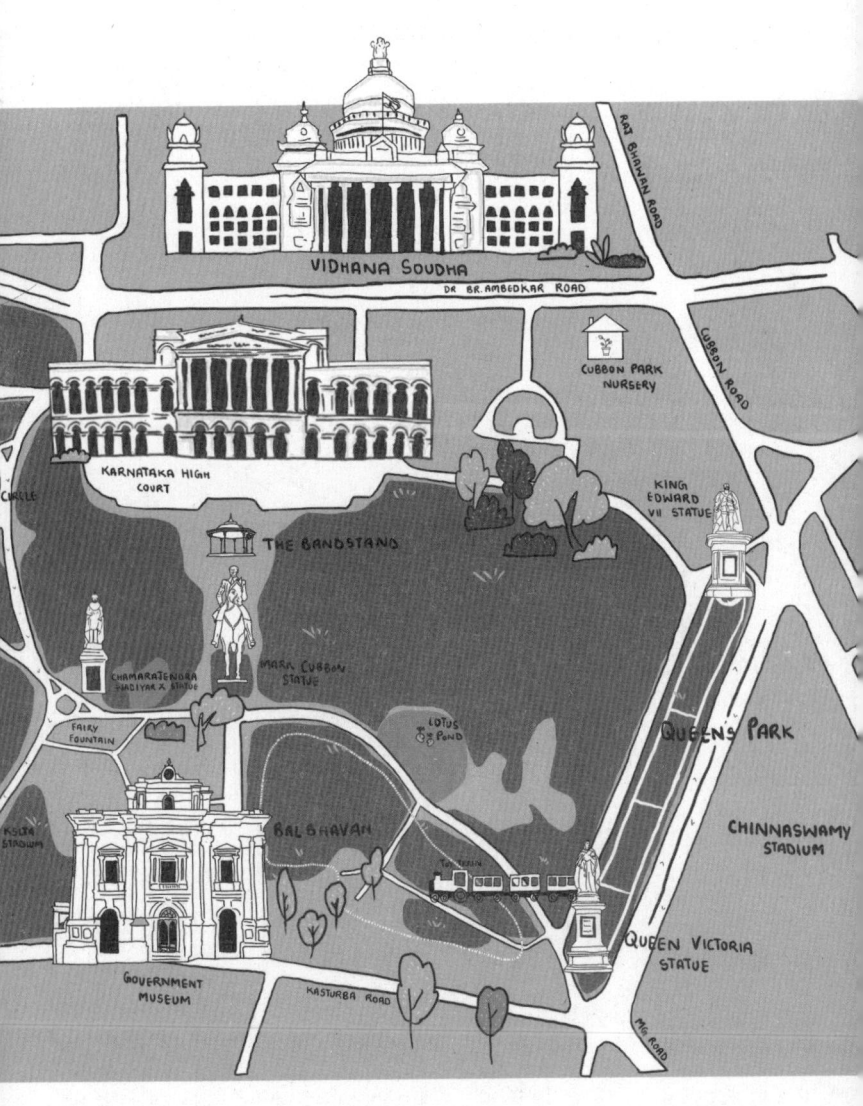

Cubbon Park: Bangalore Central

How would I describe Cubbon Park? That's easy! Central to a weekend!

—Paul Fernandes, artist, writer, designer and Bangalore's pre-eminent visual chronicler

Cubbon Park is an emotional issue for all Bangaloreans. This one space does not threaten to exclude anybody. Cubbon Park is not a tourist show-piece.

The sustainability of a city is characterised by the righteous protection of its land. Parks and open spaces are created not out of political necessity or willingness, but by sheer necessity of survival within a densely crowded and inhumane habitat.

The wild beauty of Cubbon Park is incomparable. No other city can boast of 300 acres (or is it just 100 acres?) of verdant splendour at its very heart. The battle to save Cubbon Park therefore, is a whole-hearted and unified struggle to save our habitat.

—Excerpt from 'The Battle for Cubbon Park' by Leo Saldanha, environmentalist and activist, in the November 1998 issue of *The Bangalore Monthly*

In September 1998, almost a quarter of a century ago now, a legislation passed by the Karnataka government galvanized the citizens of an entire city into extraordinary and unprecedented action. It was one of those watershed moments, when that amorphous amassment of people, passions and priorities that has earned the right to call itself a city pauses, briefly, in its ceaseless pulling in a hundred different directions at once, and coalesces spontaneously—and seemingly irrationally—into a single-pointed, high-intensity laser beam, intent on achieving a common goal.

What made this coming together of Bangalore particularly remarkable was what was at stake—not public health or safety, not a lack of water or electricity, not garbage pile-ups or potholed roads or traffic congestion (all chronic Bangalore afflictions), but 32 acres—or 44 acres, depending on how you looked at it—of a park. The people's protests of 1998 were against the government's arbitrary 'denotification' of those 32 acres, a move that stripped that parcel of land of the protection it had hitherto enjoyed under the Karnataka Government Parks (Preservation) Act of 1975, and laid it open to appropriation and redevelopment by the government and other influential parties.

What was also remarkable was the manner of the coming together. The issue brought thousands of ordinary and celebrity citizens out of their homes and into the streets, and inspired journalists across the spectrum to lay aside their differences and back the public against the establishment.

The protests went on for weeks and weeks, but never crossed the line from civil engagement into violence, or from constitutional, legal battles into vigilantism.

It is important to clarify that this was no ordinary park. This was a historic, then 128-year-old park, one of two heritage lung spaces of the city. It must also be revealed, right at the outset, that despite all their sweat, toil and tears, the citizens did not succeed in persuading the government to roll back the legislation. This story, after all, is an Indian story, which characteristically takes long and roundabout routes to a messy denouement that neither side totally loves but grudgingly accepts for the interim.

In that sense, that 1998 episode wasn't what you might call a 'victory' for the city, but one would be hard-pressed to call it a defeat, either. For that kind of inflection point in a city's history does far more than impact its future. In a million big and little ways, it also rewires its imagination. With

Ramjee Chandran

The Bangalore Monthly, the only real 'city' magazine Bangalore has had, had a great run from 1996 to 2013, with a name change along the way. It continues to celebrate and chronicle the city and its happenings, in a digital avatar, at bangalore.explocity.com

the Save Cubbon Park protests, a specific idea of what it meant to be part of this particular city took root, and a bar to live up to had been set.

*

Which begs the question: what makes Cubbon Park so important, so meaningful and so beloved? More importantly, what makes it so *central*—for that word comes up a bizarre number of times when the Park is being referenced—to the city?

Well, there is its physical location, for one. Historically, the Park lay at the intersection of two entirely different ways of life—the Bangalore Cantonment, administered by the British, and the Bengaluru Pettah*, aka City, administered by the Maharaja of Mysore—making it a no-man's land between oppressor and oppressed, soldiers and civilians, foreigners and natives, tea-drinkers and coffee-drinkers, largely church- and mosque-goers and largely temple-goers, Tamil- and Urdu-speakers and Kannada-speakers (the elite on both sides, then as now, spoke English). After Independence, when City and Cantonment were merged to create the new capital city of Mysore State, the Park became a staging area for wary rapprochement, a safe space betwixt MG Road and KG Road.

---

*Pettah was the British corruption of the Kannada word Pete, or market town, which referred to the 'native' areas around the original 16th-century town of Bengaluru.

A picture of Cubbon Park as it looked in 1870, the year of its founding. The building on the left is St Mark's Cathedral, which was founded in 1808, two years after the Bangalore Cantonment itself came into being. On the right, beyond the ornamental lamppost, is the bandstand, in its original location at Ringwood Circle.

By and by, it also became the state's administrative centre, the nucleus around which the four pillars of democracy swirled. The Judiciary, in the form of the Karnataka High Court, settled into the Attara Kacheri, the state's original administrative offices, its grounds stretching almost a kilometre along the Park's western periphery. Both houses of Legislature and the entire state cabinet moved into the Vidhana Soudha across the road. The Executive occupied the rather unimaginatively named Multi-Storeyed Building beside the Soudha. As for the Fourth Estate, it not only scattered itself in various locations around the Park's boundaries but also, crossing the imaginary lines between competing publications, met each evening to trade yarns and hot tips at the Press Club inside the Park.

And yet, amid all the chaos that surrounded it, the Park offered oases of silence and birdsong and dappled shade to those who needed it. Never entirely fenced about in its 152-year-old history, the Park became Bangalore's meeting place, sanctuary, and thoroughfare—a place the city went to and went through.

It was thus, over the years, organically and effortlessly, that Cubbon Park became central to the Bangalorean heart. A welcoming buffer zone under an open, liberal sky, a capacious green sink with an ability to subsume not only carbon dioxide but also a diversity of ideas and opinions, the Park has always been a space that carries in itself the very DNA of the city that Kempegowda built. And that's why this Bangalore institution, built of equal parts nostalgia, habit, and pure love, is the hero of this book.

Which came first? Which influences which? Was it the intrinsically liberal nature of the native Kannadigas that imbued the Park with its large-heartedness, or is it that belligerents of every stripe lost their ire within the confines of this green cathedral? That is a question for the ages, but one thing is true: the very air of Cubbon Park, its soil, its trees, its (dwindling) waters, is charged with the energy of its people—the ones that birthed it into being, the ones that watch over it from their pedestals of stone, the ones that enhanced it in small and big ways, the ones that fight for it, the ones that care for it, and the ones that visit it and revel in it and love it.

This book is as much about its people as it is about the Park. As long as Bangaloreans, old and new, carry in their hearts the spirit of these verdant, welcoming acres, and are willing to stand up to anyone or anything that threatens it, this city will have nothing to fear.

The Making of the People's Park

No small difficulties presented themselves in the selection of a suitable site, partly from objections to placing the building on any of the military parade grounds, which occupy the only approximately level portions of Bangalore, and partly from the high compensation demanded by private owners for other eligible positions. At length, however, a site was fixed on, which had originally been specially named by Sir Mark Cubbon (…) It lies immediately beyond the western extremity of the general parade ground, and so far as mere position goes, is as centrical, with reference to the populations of the Pettah on one side, and the Cantonment Bazaar and Military station on the other, as could be desired…and as year by year the trees of the 'Cubbon' Park round the Offices increase in number and size, matters will improve…

—From the essay 'Offices of the Mysore Government in Bangalore' by Lieut. Col. RH Sankey, RE, Chief Engineer, Mysore, published in *Professional Papers on Indian Engineering—Vol II (1873)*, edited by Major AM Lang

It is not obvious, unless you run or cycle here regularly, that Bangalore is in fact built on a series of granite hills. The biggest advantages of the city's position, whether we are talking about the clement all-year-round weather, the inherent immunity it enjoys from earthquakes and riverine floods, or the vast number of natural lakes that formed in the rocky depressions where the runoff from rainwater collected, are a result of its topography.

They are also the reason for its peculiar problems. The construction of the Bangalore Metro, for instance, will necessarily take longer to complete than metros in other cities because the underground sections can only be created by tunnelling through solid rock. There is an abundance of motorized two-wheelers on the streets, causing severe traffic congestion, because cycling these slopes requires more commitment than cycling across a flat city. And a heavier-than-usual downpour routinely causes homes and apartments in low-lying areas to be flooded, because many of these areas were originally lake beds (that the municipality is often negligent of keeping the city's storm drains unclogged, is another matter).

It is no wonder then that Lieutenant Colonel Richard Sankey, who served as chief engineer of Mysore between 1864 and 1877, was so hard-pressed to find a large enough piece of high, level ground on which to construct his most prestigious project—a spanking new set of Public Offices for the Mysore Administration—in the early 1860s. As it turned out, the vision of loveliness he eventually raised, the Attara Kacheri—skinny, low-slung, built in a style described as Greek neoclassical, and painted the arresting colour that the Pantone shade card lists as Pompeian Red—would endure well into the current day, as the home of the Karnataka High Court. Directly opposite the Kacheri, higher up the slope and sitting atop a grand sweep of stairs that lead to a colonnaded porch, is the awe-inspiring, neo-Dravidian, gleaming, white-granite thing of beauty that is the Vidhana Soudha, home to the state legislature since 1965.

These two iconic buildings, each representing a different age, aesthetic sensibility and political agenda, make for an arresting visual. Within that visual is contained the compelling tale of two cities—the Maharaja's Bengaluru and British Bangalore.

*

There is an apocryphal story about Kempegowda I, a chieftain of Yelahanka who, in 1537, raised a mud fort around a brand-new town that became the core of today's Bangalore. Kempegowda, so the story goes, armed with the blessings of his king, Achyutaraya, of the Vijayanagara empire, rode south on his horse from Yelahanka, looking for a suitable place to locate his new capital. At some point, the sun being fierce, he decided to take a nap in the scrubby shade of the meagre vegetation the rocky landscape afforded. Not very much later, a scuffling in the bushes having roused him from his slumber, he beheld an astonishing sight—a hound, tail tucked between his legs, was fleeing from a long-legged hare giving determined chase. 'This, then,' said a suitably awed Kempegowda to himself, 'is veerabhoomi, heroic ground. If I build my capital here, then I, the underdog, will one day be able to challenge my overlord at Vijayanagara, and send him packing.' And Kempegowda planted his flag at the spot, and built the town of Bengaluru.

As a genesis story, this one is far from unique—other Indian cities, and empires, including Vijayanagara, have similar ones. But almost 500 years later, considering the kind of status his little, relatively young town now enjoys globally, Kempegowda's instinct about veerabhoomi seems well-founded. Still, it is likely that it wasn't so much a belligerent hare, as the view at the spot, that convinced the chieftain of Yelahanka to raise a city there. Consider this: Mysore Bank Circle, at the junction of Palace Road and Kempegowda Road, lies at the centre of the northern boundary of what used to be Kempegowda's Bengaluru. It is also, at an elevation of 924 m, among the highest points on the landscape for miles.

Imagine now, therefore, this alternative, more plausible scenario, with our Kempegowda standing at that point, facing south, and looking around him. In the distance, in every direction, are high hills, affording excellent vantage points for defence. The land around where he stands is a bit up and down, but the gradients are gentle here, and there is a largish area before him that is relatively flat. Looking west, he sees the land under his feet slope away towards a natural tank—Dharmambudhi—at 904 m; towards the east, the slope is gentler. In the south, the land descends for about a kilometre, to 902 m, after which it begins to rise again. If he locates his city in this shallow bowl, it will not only be nicely contained, but will also be well provided with water, given the relative elevation of the Dharmambudhi tank. This could work, exults our Kempegowda, and planting his flag on the spot, builds the town of Bengaluru.

*

Cut to approximately 1862, when Assistant Chief Engineer Sankey, standing a mere kilometre and a half away from where Kempegowda had presumably stood 325 years before, decided that was where Mysore's new public offices would be built. A set of plans for the new offices—an expensive though desperately necessary project—had been submitted seven years earlier, in 1857, before Sankey had arrived on the scene, but they had been rejected as unsuitable. Further progress on the project had been indefinitely delayed, for an issue of a rather more pressing nature had unexpectedly arisen before the British government: the outbreak of the so-called 'Sepoy Mutiny'. Now, finally, the project had been greenlighted, and no one was keener to get it off the ground than Sankey.

What was Sankey's rush? Why did Mysore need new public offices? Thereby hangs a long and riveting tale.

On 4 May 1799, the death of Tipu Sultan rang the curtains down on the Fourth Anglo-Mysore War, the last in a series of wars fought between 1766 and 1799 between the armies of Mysore and the East India Company. It also signalled the end of any further resistance to the rise of the British in southern India.

It was Tipu's father, Hyder Ali, who had wrested power from the hereditary rulers of Mysore, the Wadiyars, in 1760. After Tipu's death, as per the terms of their pre-war agreement, the British restored the kingdom of Mysore to the Wadiyars.

One of the architects of Tipu's fall at the Battle of Seringapatam (Srirangapattana) was the young and talented Colonel Arthur Wellesley, who was appointed Governor of Mysore and Seringapatam in the aftermath of the war. Chuffed, the thirty-year-old moved into Tipu's summer palace in Seringapatam, Dariya Daulat, to begin the next phase of what would turn out to be a spectacular global military career, one that would include his defeat of Napoleon Bonaparte at the Battle of Waterloo in 1815. (Yes, it was Arthur Wellesley of Seringapatam who, in later years, would come to be known as the First Duke of Wellington!)

By 1804, having led several other successful campaigns in India, specifically against the Marathas, Arthur was beginning to tire of the country. Understandably so, for the poor man had suffered extensively, not only from a terrible fungal skin infection in the tropical climate, but also chronic diarrhoea from, well, drinking the water. In 1805, when his brother, Lord Richard Wellesley, completed his term as governor-general of India, Arthur returned with him to England, for good.

No sooner had the younger Wellesley left than the British troops still stationed at mosquito-ridden Seringapatam petitioned the twelve-year-old Maharaja of Mysore, Mummadi Krishnaraja Wadiyar (aka Krishnaraja Wadiyar III), for an alternative piece of land—near the Bengaluru Pettah, perhaps?—to establish a military station. The maharaja, in consultation with his regent, Dewan Purnaiah, granted them 9,000 acres of land to the east of the Pettah, in the environs of the centuries-old village of Halasuru. In 1806, the Bangalore Cantonment was born.

*

By no means were the British newcomers to Bengaluru Pettah. As far back as March 1791, during the Third Anglo-Mysore War, British troops led by the then governor-general, Lord Cornwallis, had stormed and captured the 17th-century citadel that lay to the south of Kempegowda's walled city. With Bengaluru, strategically located between the British southern HQ of Madras and Tipu's capital of Seringapatam as his base, Cornwallis planned his next move—the assault on Seringapatam.

A year later, Cornwallis had Tipu where he wanted him—signing a treaty whose provisions included ceding large portions of his kingdom to the British and their allies. The Bengaluru Fort, and Tipu's spare but elegant summer palace inside it, however, were restored to the Sultan, who swore he would not occupy either until he had completely destroyed the British. That day, sadly, was never to come.

In the intervening year between the fall of Bengaluru and the end of the war, British officers and troops had had ample occasion to enjoy the delights of Bengaluru Pettah. It was not surprising, therefore, that when the opportunity to build themselves a Cantonment presented itself, the area around the Pettah should be the first to come to mind.

*

Cut straight back to Mysore, circa 1810. The maharaja had just turned sixteen, and his most capable dewan, Purnaiah, who had served Mysore loyally for over three decades under three rulers—Hyder Ali, Tipu Sultan, and Mummadi himself—was keen to hand over charge of the kingdom and enjoy a well-deserved retirement. Accordingly, with the blessings of the British Resident at the Mysore court, the reins were transferred, and Purnaiah retired in 1811.

Without Purnaiah's sharp mind to aid the inexperienced young king at the helm, Mysore's administration began to slip. The Palegars, or local chieftains, who had been kept firmly in check by the dewan, began to revolt. A few bad crop seasons, coupled with a system of agricultural taxation that provided fertile ground for corruption and extortion, did not help matters. The kingdom's revenue dipped, and disgruntled peasants, particularly in the proud Shivamogga region, began to band together against the king.

In August 1830, a peasant uprising, referred to in British records as the Nagar Revolt, broke out in the Nagara region of Shivamogga. It would be almost a year before it was suppressed, and not before the maharaja had been forced to call in help from the East India Company.

Very soon after the insurrection had been quelled and a peace treaty signed, the then governor-general of India, Lord William Bentinck, citing extreme misgovernance on the part of 'this incapable and mischievous government', sent off a letter of suspension to the maharaja. With very little choice left to him, the king surrendered his authority without a murmur.

The commission set up to investigate the causes of the Nagar Revolt took another year to submit its report. One of the officers on the commission was a Lieutenant Colonel Mark Cubbon, then serving as commissary general under the Resident of Travancore.

In 1834, further to the commission's findings, Lord Bentinck made the executive decision that Mysore would thenceforth be placed under the charge of two commissioners. One he would pick himself; the other, a native counterpart, was to be nominated by the Governor of Madras. But such a native—a Mysorean who was both a man of great personal integrity held in high regard by his own people, and one who could also work well with the British—was apparently not to be found. As an alternative, two European commissioners were proposed. One was to be Mark Cubbon, and the other his predecessor in the Travancore Commissary, William Morrison. But the two men did not get along, leading Bentinck to finally appoint the more senior Morrison sole commissioner.

Fortunately for Cubbon, however, and fortunately for the kingdom of Mysore, just two months into his new appointment, Morrison was made a member of the Supreme Council of India. The post of commissioner fell vacant, and it was Cubbon who, quite naturally, was brought in to fill it. Under this new and sympathetic commissioner, who would hold the position for the next twenty-seven years, Mysore would enjoy a period of great reorganization, discipline and peace.

*

The main block (of Tipu's Palace) consisted of a long, low, ill-ventilated, ill-flavoured, ill-divided and rickety double-storeyed building, which was at once the torment of all who had to use it, and the despair of the Officers who were charged with the duty of preventing it from falling down.

—From the essay 'Offices of the Mysore Government in Bangalore', by Lieut. Col. RH Sankey, 1873

When the British moved back to the city in 1806 to build the Cantonment, their first thought was for churches and barracks and parade grounds, not administrative buildings—they were soldiers, after all, not rulers. They were also not really interested in the Pettah, that area being under the direct jurisdiction of the maharaja. And so Tipu's Palace, unoccupied since 1792, continued to lie neglected.

It was only in 1831, when control of the entire kingdom of Mysore, and with it the Bengaluru Pettah, passed into British hands, that the scouting for a suitable building or buildings to house their administrative offices began. Tipu's Palace offered itself quite naturally to the first commissioner, and was immediately accepted. For twenty-seven years,

This watercolour painting by Lieutenant James Hunter, titled *The entrance of Tippoo's Palace*, was executed in February 1792, while the Third Anglo-Mysore War raged and the British held Bengaluru Fort.

Sir Mark continued to use the crumbling palace inside the old citadel as his offices, insisting that it served very well for his own and the administration's purposes, refusing to spend public money on things he considered wasteful and unnecessary.

In that time, however, the number of administrative departments, and the number of people each of those departments employed, had increased to well beyond the capacity of the palace buildings. Administrative offices, therefore, had been set up, willy-nilly, all over the City and Cantonment, badly hampering efficiency. When Cubbon retired in 1861, the project of creating from scratch a new set of public offices for the Mysore administration finally had the chance to be critically reviewed.

Unlike Cubbon, who had arrived in India as the scion of a proud military family of old India hands, the new commissioner, Lewin Bentham Bowring, came from a civil services background. What's more, Bowring, only thirty-eight years old when he took over in 1862, was from an entirely different generation. He had very little patience with Cubbon's administrative methods, and lost no time in putting his 'modern' ideas in place.

Apart from streamlining the administration, Bowring also brought in tax and jail reform, and cleaned up to a great extent the Augean stables that were the state's audit and accounts department. But the contribution of his seven-year administration that is most relevant to us was this: in a significant departure from Sir Mark's attitude to state finances, Bowring believed implicitly that surplus revenue was not meant to be hoarded, but spent liberally on public works. Plunging into the overflowing treasury that Cubbon had built up for Mysore, he began to issue contracts for roads, bridges, tanks, sanitation, conservancy, and, yes, the desperately needed public offices.

And that's why—here we come, finally, to the end of our very long answer to a very simple question—Chief Engineer Sankey was in such a great rush to find the perfect site to begin building. In the end, he settled on a spot that Cubbon himself had once suggested, just a little to the east of the 'High Grounds', the highest point in the Cantonment at 940 m, where Cubbon's own residence (today the Karnataka Raj Bhavan, where the governor resides) stood. Sankey's spot, only 15 m lower, would ensure that the building would always remain safe and dry, but because of the 'peculiar conformation of the ground', it was not possible for him to make the building as elevated as he would have hoped, or align it as squarely as he would have liked to the parade ground it fronted. To make matters more vexatious, the ground 'sloped away so rapidly' from the level area that Sankey was forced to design a building that was 'unduly long with reference to its breadth'. No matter, everyone would simply have to make their peace with that.

The new Mysore Public Offices were inaugurated in 1868. The building itself was referred to as the Attara

A 1918 postcard showing the front entrance of the Attara Kacheri, which then faced Cubbon Park.

Kacheri, or 'Eighteen Departments', based on the system of administration that had been followed in Mysore since the 17th century, when Maharaja Chikkadevaraja Wadiyar, impressed with the concept, had borrowed it from the Mughals.

There was one last, small, but most important, detail to be seen to. To the British, an administrative building, grand as it may be, is only an administrative building, but place it within a 'park', a large area of manicured lawns and gardens and fountains and soaring trees and sweeping driveways, and it suddenly transforms into a stately 'manor house'. And that's why Sankey also designed, over the ground that 'sloped away rapidly' in front of the new Public Offices, and the swathe of land that rose behind it, towards Cubbon's house and grounds, an extensive 100-acre park.

Owing both to its elevation and its central position, that Park, inaugurated in 1870, would go on to become one of the city's most beloved green spaces—a jewel located both at its head and its heart. And even though it didn't start out with that name, and although different people along the way would try to give it different names, one, and only one, would stick—Cubbon Park.

People of the Park

The First 100 Years

The Birthers

The Park is named after Sir Mark Cubbon, Chief Commissioner of Mysore, and covers over a hundred acres. It contains the Public Offices, built in 1868 by Col (now Sir) Richard Sankey, before which is an equestrian statue of Sir Mark Cubbon, the band promenade, and the Government Museum. In addition to carriage drives and broad promenades, there are many tortuous paths and shady nooks which all help to provide a pleasant retreat, whether for pleasure or rest.

—From the caption of an 1890's picture of Cubbon Park, part of the Curzon Collection's 'Souvenir of Mysore' album

IF A GOOD BEGINNING IS THE KEY TO FUTURE SUCCESS, THERE could have been no better beginning for Cubbon Park than the grit, guts and integrity of the three men who, in their own ways, brought it into existence. Nothing, however, was quite straightforward about the relationship each had with the Park, or vice versa.

The first, Commissioner Cubbon, long dead by the time the Park was born, had precious little to do with it. Yet he was the only one fortunate enough to make it his posthumous home—for 152 years, and counting. The second, Richard Sankey, dreamt the Park up as an elaborate setting for his grandest creation, the Attara Kacheri. Yet, his best-known successes came not from the drafting table but the battlefield. The third, Richard Meade, was the only one around during the Park's babyhood; he was the parent who patiently taught it to walk before it could run. But he is also the one most seldom acknowledged when the Park is mentioned, and then, only as a barely there footnote.

And yet, in a wholly insidious, wholly wonderful way, it was these men who set the course that the Park would follow.

THE COMMISSIONER
Sir Mark of the Park

Were Mysore in rebellion tomorrow, his (Cubbon's) word would be sufficient to suppress it, and such has ever been the respect entertained for him and the influence of his salutary policy, that no army was required to overawe the millions subject to his rule.

—From a report in the 19th-century *Bangalore Herald*, on Cubbon's retirement as Commissioner of Mysore and Coorg

I have not words to express how greatly my feelings were shocked when the news of General Cubbon's death was announced to

me. In him I have lost a valued friend and well-wisher, and the public services one of its most honourable members.

—Mummadi Krishnaraja Wadiyar, writing to General James Stuart Fraser, former Resident of Mysore

LUSHINGTON, BRIGGS, MORRISON, CUBBON, BOWRING, Meade, Saunders, Gordon…to most Bangaloreans, at least five of those seven names almost certainly will not ring a bell. Yet it was these seven men who, over the half century that Mysore was ruled directly by the British in the 19th century, served as all-powerful commissioners of the state. Of the two names that may have some recall, one is Bowring's, if only because there is a hospital and a gentleman's club, both in the erstwhile Cantonment, that carry his name. The other, memorialized equally in a neighbourhood on the City side—Cubbonpet, a main street on the Cantonment side, Cubbon Road, and

https://www.hipstamp.com/listing/isle-of-man-lieutenant-general-sir-mark-cubbon-3v-1985-mnh-sc291-293/45963913

In 1985, the Isle of Man issued a first day cover and a set of postage stamps to commemorate the bicentenary of its most famous son, Sir Mark Cubbon. The 22p stamp, shown here, depicts Sir Mark as Commissioner of Mysore.

in the sprawling park that straddled the divide—is Mark Cubbon's.

Sir Mark came out to India from his native Isle of Man quite late in life, at the age of twenty-five, and moved south the very next year, as part of the 2nd Madras Battalion. In this, he was not without precedent; his maternal uncle, Mark Wilks, had joined the Madras Army at eighteen. Over the next three decades, Cubbon proceeded to distinguish himself in both military and civil appointments across the peninsula, developing on the way a deep understanding and appreciation of native Indian soldiers and their traditions. In 1834, via a series of fortunate occurrences, he was appointed Commissioner of Mysore and Coorg.

There was perhaps an element of family destiny in Cubbon's association with Mysore, for Mark Wilks had himself fought alongside General James Stuart in 1799 in the final storming of Seringapatam, and served as the British Resident of Mysore between 1803 and 1808. After his return to England in 1809, he had also published one of the first histories of Mysore and the Wadiyars, the three-volume *Historical Sketches of the South of India*.

The Mysore that Wilks' nephew inherited was riddled with problems—deep-rooted corruption, rampant crime, nepotism towards certain castes, a lack of separation between military and police, and, most shockingly, the absence of a universal code of law, which had allowed a culture of corporal punishment, mutilation and torture to

The palatial residence of Sir Mark, in a photograph from 1894. It was purchased by his successor, Lord Bowring, in the 1860s, to serve as the Residency, the official home of the Commissioner of Bangalore. Since 1964, it has functioned as Karnataka's Raj Bhavan, the official residence of the governor of the state.

flourish. To add to his woes were poorly paid, and therefore disgruntled, soldiers and administrative staff, a treasury bled dry by rapacious officials, and a bureaucratic tower of Babel—government documents were written, according to the whim of the presiding official, in Urdu, Hindi, Persian, Kannada or Marathi. But the most urgent issue the new commissioner had before him was the quelling of various insurrections, like the Nagar Revolt, that routinely erupted across the land.

It was a mammoth task, but Cubbon's vast experience in southern India and his understanding of the Indian mind helped him transform the landscape of Mysore's governance in the twenty-seven years of his rule. For a code of law, he drew upon his uncle Wilks' system, which the latter had created in consultation with Arthur Wellesley. Raising a police force in the very year of his taking over, he confined the language of official documents to Kannada and Marathi. To make them harder to corrupt, he raised the pay of the native horsemen and created a force of close to 4,000 horses. Apart from improving roads all over the state, he pushed hard for a railway line connecting Bangalore to Madras and the rest of the peninsula, though that project would only come to fruition after his death, when the first train steamed into Cantonment station from Jolarpettai (in present-day Tamil Nadu) in 1864. He also—hold your breath—commissioned the very first Kannada translation of the Bhagavad Gita in 1849, and, nine years later, the first Kannada-English dictionary.

Inordinately fond of horses, this bachelor-for-life maintained a personal stable of sixty fine steeds on the 90-acre grounds of his residence at Bangalore's High Grounds, and persuaded the British government to improve the local breed instead of depending so desperately on Arabian stock. In 1839, he founded the Agro-Horticultural Society to introduce new and better varieties of crops to Mysore, and had Tipu's beloved Lalbagh transferred to its care. Lalbagh would go on to become one of the country's premier botanical gardens, the nursery of most of the exotic species that grow so wild and beautiful in today's Cubbon Park.

As commissioner, Cubbon had absolute power, but far from corrupting him absolutely, it made this vicar's son hyper-aware of his responsibilities. Even as his new and improved systems of irrigation, agriculture, taxation and revenue collection filled British and Mysore coffers, his lean, mean administration, which employed mostly Indians, cost the exchequer no more than 13,000 pounds a year.

Sir Mark retired in 1861, at the ripe old age of eighty-five, and then only because of ill health. On his way home, his first such journey in sixty years, this genial Manxman, who had even managed to build a cordial relationship with the maharaja he had deposed, passed away on board ship at Suez. He lies buried at the Maughold vicarage where he spent his childhood, hailed as 'the greatest man this island has produced for centuries back'.

*

The news of Sir Mark's death expectedly plunged Mysore into grief. A series of animated discussions regarding a fitting memorial for the great man presumably followed. In the end, it was decided that only an equestrian statue, cast entirely, and expensively, in bronze, would do Cubbon's immense contributions justice. What's more, it would be executed by one of the most celebrated sculptors of the age, Baron Carlo Marochetti, who counted among his works the four bronze lions at the base of Nelson's column at Trafalgar Square, and the equestrian statue of Richard the Lionheart at London's Houses of Parliament.

The long journey from the Marochetti studio at London's posh Sydney Mews to the Parade Ground in Bangalore's South Parade (today's MG Road), in an age before the Suez Canal existed, must have been an exhausting one for Sir Mark's statue. Once there, it was unveiled with great pomp and ceremony by his successor, Lord Bowring, in 1866. Only four years later, however, Sir Mark's statue was on the move again. This time, mercifully, the journey was a much shorter one, a few hundred metres west, where it was installed at the imposing entrance of the just-completed Attara Kacheri.

For a century and a half, the statue of Sir Mark stood unmolested in the Park that bore his name, watching the city that was his home grow and flourish. Until 2020, when another exigency forced the peripatetic statue to up sticks again, and move a hundred metres east. (Find out why on page 150).

There it stands today, flanked by stately copperpod trees, a symbol of globalization from a time before the word was invented, bringing together in itself the art of an Italian-French sculptor, the unstinting efforts of a British Commissioner who gave so many years of his life to tightening and tidying up the administration of a little Cantonment town half a world away from where he grew up, and the enduring love and respect of a southern Indian people.

THE ENGINEER
There's More to Sankey Than a Tank-ey

No man in my opinion ever better earned the V. C. (Victoria Cross) than did Major Sankey. In the performance of his duty he exposed himself to almost certain death, setting a brilliant example of courage to the men who were engaged with him at the fort (of Jumalpur); and I may add with much truth that his services on that occasion contributed greatly to the capture of the place...

—General Charles Metcalfe MacGregor, quoted in *Addiscombe: Its Heroes and Men of Note* by Colonel HM Vibart, published 1894

I think Sankey was the most brilliant officer of the Madras Engineers during the last half century. He was a born leader of men (...) he deserved and obtained the confidence and affection of the officers and men who worked under him. He was an accomplished painter in oils and watercolours, enjoyed a run with the hounds at Ooty and a game of polo at Bangalore, he was a deep thinker and a diligent reader, a charming companion...

—Sir Harry Prendergast, VC, GCB, quoted in the obituary to Sankey carried in the June 1909 issue of the *Royal Engineers Journal*

FEW KANNADIGAS WOULD HAVE REASON TO BE ACQUAINTED with County Tipperary in faraway Ireland if not for a popular British music hall song, 'It's a Long Way to

Tipperary'. A favourite with British soldiers during the First World War, it inspired a chartbusting Kannada version—'Namma Tipparahalli balu doora'—by the beloved Kannada poet, playwright, punster, and overall creative genius TP Kailasam, who first heard the original as a student of geology in London.

Fewer Kannadigas, or Bengalureans, are aware that it was a man from the self-same County Tipperary who designed some of this city's most iconic buildings and spaces and reservoirs. This man, another genius with an interest in geology (his collection of prehistoric plant fossils from Nagpur lies somewhere in the bowels of the British Museum) was Sir Richard Hieram Sankey.

It wasn't engineering that was on Sankey's mind, however, when, as a young lad of sixteen, he first mounted the steps of Croydon's East India Company Military Seminary, an institution whose stated mission was to train young officers to serve in the Company's private army in India. Following in the proud military tradition of his mother's family, he simply wanted to be a soldier. But his natural bent towards the mechanical and the artistic was soon noticed, and he won his first commission with the Madras Sappers*. After a brief period of training in military

---

*Now known as the Madras Engineer Group (MEG) this proud corps of engineers, founded in 1780, is the oldest in the Indian Army. The regiment has been headquartered in Bangalore since 1834, well before Sankey was recruited.

engineering, he proceeded to India in 1848, still nineteen, to take up his duties.

After a meandering journey through various positions in Mercara (Madikeri), Nagpur and Madras, Sankey was called up to Calcutta in 1857 to serve as under-secretary with the Public Works Department (PWD). Soon after, though, with the rumblings among Indian soldiers in Bengal finally exploding in Meerut into the great 'Mutiny', the twenty-eight-year-old rode out to do his part in quelling it, as Captain of the Calcutta Cavalry Volunteers. He acquitted himself very honourably for his side, both as engineer and soldier, constructing defensive works like entrenchments, causeways, roads and bridges across the Ganga and the Yamuna, and playing a key role in vital campaigns responsible for breaking the Siege of Lucknow. For his 'great and successful exertions', Sankey was recommended by his Commander (unsuccessfully, as it turns out) for the Victoria Cross.

The multidimensional engineer-officer Richard Sankey, who gave Bangalore, among other things, so many of its most recognizable 19th-century buildings.

In 1861, the year of Sir Mark Cubbon's death, Bangalore got Sankey to itself, as part of the engineering corps of

Mysore, whence he proceeded to employ both sides of his fine brain for the benefit of Bangalore Cantonment. One of the first things this passionate hydrologist did was to set up a never-before Irrigation Department to deal scientifically with the existing tank system, which greatly interested him. His systematic survey of the city's old tanks led him to construct weirs, repair and improve channels connecting tanks that drained into others, and create separate channels for drainage. He also designed a reservoir to supplement the growing city's insatiable water needs. That reservoir—Sankey Tank, the only landmark in the city named after him—would not be completed until 1882, five years after he had moved on from here.

Elevated to chief engineer in 1864, Sankey celebrated by designing not only the lovely Attara Kacheri building—and the park around it—but also St Andrew's Kirk, the Scottish Presbyterian church on Cubbon Road, with its Gothic flourishes and stained-glass windows. When the Viceroy, Lord Mayo, was assassinated in Port Blair in 1872, Sankey designed the Mayo Hall, which is located at the junction of MG Road and Residency Road and now houses the City Civil Courts, as a memorial. In parallel, he designed the stately two-storeyed Government Museum on Kasturba Road, to house the second oldest museum in south India.

After his thirteen-year stint as Chief Engineer of Mysore, Sankey moved on to serve in the Madras PWD,

When the Mayo Hall, a Sankey-designed building, was inaugurated in 1883, the *Bangalore District Gazetteer* was fulsome in its appreciation. 'The building, in elevation,' it noted, 'is remarkable for its composition of architrave and pedimented windows, varied with key-storied arches, beautifully executed consoles, balustraded ledges and typical Greek cornice.'

designing the seaside city's famous Marina, and redoing its botanical gardens. Returning to his native Tipperary after his retirement in 1883, he took on his most onerous appointment yet—chairman of Ireland's Board of Works, which involved the building and management of civil and military offices, drainage systems, harbours, schools, and more. His favourite part of the demanding job, as can be imagined, was the care of two large parks in Dublin, which he unfailingly made time to visit at least once a week.

In one of those parks—Phoenix Park—there is a simple stone slab, half-hidden by the grass amidst a circle of trees, that attests it was this aesthetically minded engineer who planted them in 1894. If you happen to visit Phoenix Park and wish to pay your respects to the creative genius who gave us the priceless gift of Cubbon Park, ask for Sankey's Wood, and someone will guide you there.

THE OTHER COMMISSIONER
The Famous Deeds of Richard Meade

> *In these circumstances, it was, doubtless, considered important that the officer selected for the post of ad interim administrator should (…) (1) be one of proved ability in guiding and influencing native rulers and their councillors; (2) have wide experience of both English and native administrations; (3) have an open mind; (4) be tolerably pachydermatous; (5) be strong enough to withstand undue pressure from vested interests, to deal justly between the sometimes conflicting claims of European and native… the new Chief Commissioner, whoever he was to be, was promised a somewhat lively time.*
>
> —From *General Sir Richard Meade and the Feudatory States of Central and Southern India* by Thomas Henry Thornton, published 1898

ANY HISTORY OF CUBBON PARK, INCLUDING THE SHORT ONE on the signboards in the Park itself, acknowledge that it began life in 1870 as Meade's Park. By 1873, however, the Park had been rechristened. Of Meade himself, no acknowledgement was to be found thereafter, whether in the Park or anywhere else in the city. A regrettable omission, for General Meade, despite serving here only briefly, was hugely influential in setting the course for the future political history of Mysore under the maharajas.

Arriving in India in 1838 as a lad of seventeen, Richard Meade enlisted in the infantry division of the Bengal Army. For almost two decades, he led a busy and productive life, well-liked by both peers and senior officers, but with no real opportunity to prove himself.

Everything changed with the Revolt of 1857. At the time, Meade was Brigade-Major of the Gwalior Contingent, a force maintained by the Scindia of Gwalior, comprising 'sepoys' (Indian soldiers) led by British officers. When the Gwalior Contingent rose up in revolt, Meade escaped by the skin of his teeth. He was back less than a year later, however, escorting the Scindia safely back to his palace and successfully parleying with the rebels for a peaceful surrender. Then, tasked with bringing to justice the rebels still in hiding, particularly the elusive Tantia Tope, who was responsible for the massacre of Europeans in Kanpur, he went after Tope, ran him to the ground, and hanged him mercilessly.

That made him very unpopular among the Indian revolutionaries, but to his own superiors, Meade was now a superstar. What made him even more valuable was that he was seen by many Indians he worked with as a fair, if firm, representative of the Empire. In 1861, he was appointed political agent for Central India, a sensitive post if there ever was one. He served in that position for the next eight years, earning the respect of the Indian princes in the region and cementing his position as an acceptable interlocutor for both sides.

Meanwhile, in Mysore, the aging maharaja, Mummadi Krishnaraja Wadiyar, adopted his grandson Chamarajendra as his heir, and continued to harangue the British administration to restore his kingdom to him. Since 1858, when the British Crown had taken direct charge of India in the aftermath of the rebellion, his petitions had been addressed to the queen herself. In 1866, to the great joy of Mysoreans, the queen signed a royal fiat directing the viceroy to restore Mysore to its hereditary rulers. The Rendition was due to happen in 1881, when the young heir turned eighteen.

Predictably, this announcement led to a great deal of disquiet among the Europeans on the future of Mysore and the possibility of 'a return to barbarism'. To add to the general fluster, the Commissioner of Mysore, Lewin Bowring, chose to retire from the Indian Civil Service in 1870.

Bowring's retirement, at such a delicate stage in the proceedings at Mysore, put the viceroy, Lord Mayo, in a rather large pickle. Casting about for a replacement who was not only experienced but also capable of gaining the maharaja's trust, vital for setting the stage for a peaceful transition of power, he lit on Meade, quite the legend as far as his successes with Indian princes were concerned.

It was in the year that Meade took over, 1870, that the 100-acre park designed by Richard Sankey around the Attara Kacheri was completed. In honour of the new commissioner, it was named Meade's Park.

To his own surprise, Meade, who had been most reluctant to move out of central India, enjoyed his new assignment in the agreeable Bangalore Cantonment very much indeed. He also got on well with the boy king, Chamarajendra, and took a great interest in his education. The two would keep up a warm correspondence well after Meade had moved on from Mysore.

Meade continued the good work of commissioners before him, extending the railway lines, laying roads and irrigation canals,

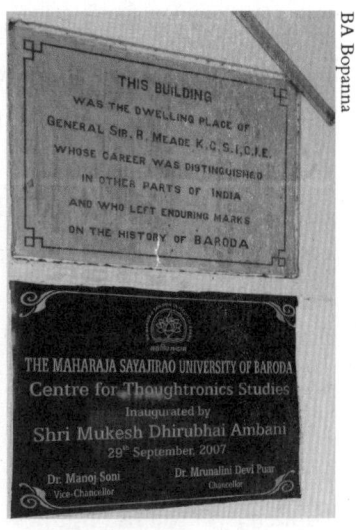

Commissioner Richard Meade, who served for forty-three years in various capacities across India, has been largely forgotten by the history books. A small but notable exception is this commemorative plaque on the front wall of the erstwhile British Residency of Baroda, now part of the Maharaja Sayajirao University.

The Birthers } 41

improving schools and education. But his most significant legacy was the report he submitted to the British government on the thorny question of whether Mysore was capable of sustaining the kind of elaborate, expensive, 'anglicized' administration that the British had pursued there, *without* Europeans in charge. After all, went the reasoning, it was the 'patriarchal system' (read: the whims of the king in power) that was 'best adapted to a native state', so it was best for the British to simply withdraw from Mysore and allow it to fall back into its old ways.

In his report, Meade unequivocally rubbished both—the racist stereotypes, and British excuses to dodge their responsibilities. 'The patriarchal system in a native state,' he wrote, 'is a synonym for anarchy and corruption…the closing years of Mysore should witness—not disorganisation in the vain pursuit of a phantom system of native administration—but a thorough consolidation of what has already been done, to the end that the province may be handed over to His Highness the Maharaja in perfect order.'

Meade's word sealed the deal. Over the next decade, a series of commissioners would work with Indian officers, more and more of whom came to be employed in the administration, to create as perfect a launching pad as was possible for the new king.

Meade's own hope for a long innings at Mysore would be thwarted, however. In September 1873, he was called away to Baroda for another delicate assignment—investigating charges of maladministration against the Gaekwad. Very soon after he had departed, the name of Meade's Park was changed to Cubbon Park, and Meade was erased, not maliciously but pretty definitively, from public memory.

In 1927, during the celebration of Chamarajendra's son and successor Nalvadi Krishnaraja Wadiyar's (aka Krishnaraja Wadiyar IV) silver jubilee, a more formal name change was effected—the Park was named after the maharaja's father, Meade's boy-king. But despite the welcome arches at the Park entrances displaying the name—Chamarajendra Park—for several years now, it is only the name of the first Commissioner of Mysore, Mark Cubbon, that has endured.

How would General Meade feel about that? Since, according to his biographer, Thomas Henry Thornton, he fulfilled the condition of being 'tolerably pachydermatous', probably not very much at all. For the Park itself, however, the association with Commissioner Meade, even if only in name, can only be counted as fortuitous—when the man who oversaw its earliest days himself epitomised 'bridging the gap', how could the Park do otherwise?

The Watchers

I do not know why government officials have so much love for colonial era rulers. The world over, imperialists' statues, like those of Lenin and Stalin, are being torn down, and here we want to restore Victoria's statue. This is a serious assault on our sensibilities and we demand nothing less than moving the statue, along with two others, to a museum.

—Vatal Nagaraj, former MLA and Kannada activist,
in a report in the *Bangalore Mirror*,
published 15 April 2014

WHICH LUMINARIES A CITY CHOOSES TO HONOUR WITH full-size statues in its premier public spaces can tell you a thing or two about that city and its people. Are the most prominent pedestal-toppers rulers, politicians, religious leaders, soldiers, movie stars, sportspeople, entrepreneurs, litterateurs, scientists or social reformers? Are a variety of social groups represented? Does the city choose to erase those parts of its history it considers repugnant, or does it move forward with a calm acceptance of what has been, acknowledging all the influences that have shaped it?

As with so many other questions about Bangalore and Bangaloreans, Cubbon Park is a good place to seek answers.

For close to a century, five statues have shared space companionably in the Park. Of the five, two—Chamarajendra Wadiyar X, Maharaja of Mysore at the time of the Park's birthing, and the legendary K Seshadri Iyer, Mysore's longest-serving dewan—represent the City; and two—Queen Victoria, self-styled Empress of India, and her son, Edward VII, who succeeded her—the Cantonment. The fifth, Sir Mark Cubbon, much like the Park itself, straddles the divide between the two sides.

What is remarkable about this specific set of grandees, given that it was political pushes and pulls that originally had a hand in their selection, is that not one of them has been judged particularly unfavourably by history. What's more, despite all of them being politicians in whom a great deal of power was invested, none of them is a polarizing figure; instead, each is seen as a fair-minded moderate who truly meant to do well by the people over whom he or she held sway.

It is a fanciful thought, but could it be the continuing presence of these specific personages, and the values they stood for, that have shaped Cubbon Park into the wholesome space it is?

THE EMPRESS
Queen Vic's Bailiwick

> *We hereby announce to the Native Princes of India that all treaties, engagements made with them by or under the authority of the Honourable East India Company are by us accepted, and will be scrupulously maintained... We desire no extensions of our present territorial possessions... We shall respect the rights, dignity and honour of Native Princes as our own...*

—Extract from Queen Victoria's Proclamation, issued following the transfer of power to the Crown, read out by Lord Canning at the Allahabad durbar on 1 November 1858

Well over a century after her passing, the once-Empress of India continues to reign over a main Bangalore promenade named after the father of the nation. But, in what feels like poetic justice, she is largely obscured for most of the year by the verdant foliage around her.

THE QUEEN STANDS AT THE WESTERN END OF THE ERSTWHILE South Parade (in other words, at the MG Road entrance to the Park), the main promenade of both the 20th-century Bangalore Cantonment and the city today. She wears a cape and robe embroidered with roses, and, over her left shoulder, the cross-body sash signifying the Order of the Garter, a medieval English order of chivalry. In her upturned left hand, she holds an orb, and in her right, the royal sceptre. Her famous hauteur in place, she looks down her imperial nose at the much smaller statue of Mahatma Gandhi in the park across the street. (Ironically enough, the piece of land that she stands on was, when she was first installed here, part of the City; Gandhi stands squarely on what was the Cantonment side.)

To tease the folds of her voluminous skirts, and the ties and tassels that secure her cape, so delicately and skilfully out of marble was clearly no mean task. But then, the sculptor picked to execute the statue, Sir Thomas Brock, was no ordinary talent.

For a monarch who had never visited India, despite ruling it indirectly for sixty-three years and directly for forty-three, the Queen was held in rather high esteem by her Indian subjects, or at least, by the maharajas and maharanis who ruled them. Soon after her death in 1901, committees came up in every British dominion, as they did in Bangalore, to discuss what kind of memorial should be raised to her. A statue, it was decided, would be most appropriate. (There was nothing particularly original about this idea—no less than fifty statues of the queen were commissioned by India alone. Only five, including the one in Cubbon Park, still stand; all the others were pulled down or moved after Independence). It was also decided that the funds required—approximately Rs 15,000—would be raised by public subscription. But with only Rs 10,000 having been collected over six months—a fact that left the British red-faced—the maharaja stepped in to make good the difference.

The Wadiyars of Mysore had good reason to be favourably disposed towards the queen. In 1831, the East India Company (EIC) had wrested Mysore from Mummadi Krishnaraja Wadiyar on flimsy and not-entirely-defensible charges of misgovernance. Over the decades, the deposed king had sent off dozens of unsuccessful petitions to commissioners and governor-generals, requesting for the restoration of his kingdom, but in vain. In 1865, when Mummadi, who did not have sons of his own, adopted his three-year-old grandson, Chamarajendra, as his heir, the British, who had happily assumed that Mysore would permanently pass to them on the king's death, were thrown into a tizzy. There was a great temptation to trot out the old Doctrine of Lapse, which disallowed adopted children from being heirs, even though it had proved, in the past, to be very unpopular with native princes.

That was when the queen decided to get involved. The

rumblings of the Revolt of 1857 had been heard loudly and clearly in Buckingham Palace and the British Houses of Parliament, and lively debates now preceded every decision taken on India. Liberal MPs, staunchly against the Doctrine of Lapse being enforced, warned that there was nothing to be gained by antagonizing Mysore, which had stayed loyal and calm through the Revolt mainly owing to the efforts of the maharaja, as reported by Commissioner Mark Cubbon himself. Convinced, the queen issued a royal order in 1866, accepting the adoption of an heir to the Mysore throne, and directing the Viceroy of India to restore the kingdom to the Wadiyars in 1881, once Chamarajendra attained maturity.

It was Chamarajendra's son, Nalvadi Krishnaraja, who, twenty years later, put in a personal donation of Rs 5,000 to ensure that the statue of the queen was completed. The queen's own favourite sculptor in her youth, Baron Carlo Marochetti (who executed the statue of Sir Mark), being long dead, it was Sir Thomas Brock, all the rage at the time in London, who was commissioned for the job. The statue arrived in India in July 1905, and was installed on its granite pedestal, but would not be unveiled until February 5 the next year, when Victoria's grandson, the then Prince of Wales, George Frederick Ernest Albert, dropped in for a visit.

For George, who would go on to become King George V in 1910, and return to India in 1911 for the famous Delhi Durbar, the four-month-long India tour of 1905-06 was largely an unveil-yet-another-statue-of-Grandma whirlwind: apart from the one in Cubbon Park, he would unveil her likenesses in Calcutta, Rangoon, Madras and Karachi.

Pedestal plaque recording the unveiling of the statue of Queen Victoria by her grandson and the future Emperor of India, George V. During his twenty-six-year reign (1910-36), the Indian Independence movement came well and truly into its own.

As for Sir Thomas Brock, his most famous work, another memorial to the queen at London, was yet to come, even though he had had it all designed in the year of her death. The one-of-its-kind monument, a labour of love, was finally completed in 1924. Simply called the Victoria Memorial, this elaborate 82-feet-tall monument stands right opposite the Buckingham Palace. It is part of the mandatory touristy pictures of a great many visitors to London from Bangalore, most of whom haven't the foggiest idea that they have a true-blue 'Thomas Brock' back in their own city.

THE EMPEROR
King Edward, a Fine Old Bird

Farewell to India

13th March, 1876—Just this day 17 weeks ago the Serapis cast anchor in Bombay. The Prince has (since then) travelled 7600 miles by land and 2300 miles by sea, knows more Chiefs than all the Viceroys and governors together and has seen more of the country in the time than any living man.

—From *The Prince of Wales' Tour of India—A Diary in India* (1877) by William Howard Russell, Honorary Private Secretary to His Royal Highness, The Prince of Wales

THE QUEEN'S PARK, WHICH RUNS ALONG A STRETCH OF THE Queen's Road from the Bal Bhavan entrance of Cubbon Park all the way to Cubbon Road, is a sort of foyer to the main Park, a slim, long stretch of manicured lawns lined with *Polyalthia longifolia* , or mast trees (the tall, long-leafed, straight-trunked trees popularly, and erroneously, referred to as Ashoka trees) and ringed around by a walking track. This park is bookended by two statues—Queen Victoria holds up one end of it, and her son and heir, Edward VII, gamely does his part on the other.

As mentioned before, it was Edward's son, George Frederick, who had unveiled his grandmother's statue in the Park in 1906. Edward would get his own pedestal only in 1919, when George was reigning as King George V. But with the king not expected to visit Bangalore anytime soon, the job of unveiling the statue fell to the viceroy, Lord Chelmsford.

The statue itself had been sculpted by Leonard Jennings, an English sculptor who had briefly taken up a commission in India as a young man, teaching at the Calcutta School of Art. Jennings was a busy man—he fought for his country in both World Wars, and his great love of horses and the hunt saw him 'riding to hounds' at every opportunity. His artistic career continued alongside, however, with most of his public commissions coming from India.

The statue of Edward VII, every detail of costume and face finely delineated and ready to be shipped to Bangalore, photographed in 1914 at sculptor Leonard Jennings' studio in Chelsea, London.

Unlike his mother Victoria, Edward had actually visited India, way back in 1875, when he was Prince of Wales, becoming the first British royal to set foot here after the Crown had taken over in 1858. He could not have guessed it then, but it would be another twenty-six years before he became king—he had the misfortune to be heir to a queen who would rule for almost sixty-four years. Edward's 'playboy prince' lifestyle didn't win him any brownie points with his mother, either—in fact, she partly blamed him for his father, Prince Albert's death (from what was most likely typhoid), following the latter's distress over Edward's brief romantic entanglement with an actress.

The maternal antipathy ensured that the crown prince was kept firmly out of state affairs until he was past fifty. But it did not stop 'Bertie' (Edward was christened Albert Edward), in his stylish tweeds and Homburg hats and penchant for black ties with dinner jackets (the usual fashion was white tie and tails), from being loved by all who knew him, including politicians with conflicting ideologies.

During the course of his four-month tour of India, the genial Prince of Wales travelled extensively, and would have covered even more ground in south India and probably even come to Bangalore if an outbreak of cholera in these parts hadn't forced him to stick to the coasts. Fair-minded by nature, he was distressed at the kind of treatment British officers often meted out to Indians, remarking, in his letters home: 'Because a man has a black face and a different religion from our own, there is no reason why he should be treated as a brute.' At least one Resident in a princely state was sacked because of his reports, and several others pulled up and reprimanded.

That kind of sentiment on the part of the prince ensured that Indians took him to their hearts. The success of the tour, among other things, prompted Prime Minister Benjamin Disraeli to suggest that the queen be addressed thenceforth as 'Empress of India'. Although the liberals in the British Parliament grumbled about the grandiose title, the queen herself liked it, and adopted it on 1 May 1876. Every British monarch after her—including Edward, who despite the queen's worst fears, became a universally popular ruler who brought the shine back into the British monarchy—would continue to use the title, all the way until 22 June 1948.

Those titles—Empress of India, Emperor of India—persist to this day on the pedestals at either end of Queen's Park, inscribed in the four principal languages of 20th-century Bengaluru and Bangalore—English, Kannada, Tamil and Urdu.

Translated into English, the Urdu legend reads: 'Edward VII, King of Great Britain and Ireland and Emperor of India 1901 to 1910. Erected by public subscription 1914.' The unveiling, however, would have to wait until 1919.

THE PRIME MINISTER
That Grand Old Sire, Seshadri Iyer

> *Among the initiatives associated with him (K. Seshadri Iyer) are the early negotiations for setting up of the Indian Institute of Science as well as the power station at Sivasamudram. That both these initiatives became reality after his death is a reflection of the fact that the tradition of modernism in Bangalore cannot be reduced to any single icon, but was built into the bureaucracy as a whole with the support of the royal family.*
>
> —From *Bengaluru, Bangalore, Bengaluru: Imaginations and Their Times*, edited by Narendar Pani, Sindhu Radhakrishna and Kishor G Bhat, 2008

> *(I) settled down at the (Government Arts) college, where I found myself enjoying my studies…I also made full use of the State Central Library in Cubbon Park. I stopped there every day on the way back from college to the hostel (on MG Road), and read all the books I could lay my hands on.*
>
> —Siddalingaiah, acclaimed Dalit Kannada poet, in his autobiography *A Word with You, World*, translated from the Kannada by SR Ramakrishna

IF THE BRITISH ROYALS STAND GUARD OVER THE CANTONMENT entrances to the Park, it is Mysore's longest-serving dewan, Kumarapuram Seshadri Iyer, who welcomes those who prefer the Hudson Circle entrance on the City side. His statue stands in the middle of a vast rose garden in front of the eponymous Seshadri Iyer Memorial Hall, a gracious building of a rather unusual shape, resplendent in Pompeian red.

Like many dewans of Mysore, Seshadri Iyer was not native to the kingdom. Born in Palghat in the then Madras Presidency, he went to school in Cochin, Calicut and Trivandrum before graduating his BA with flying colours from Presidency College, Madras. At twenty-three, he accepted an appointment as Judicial Secretary in the government of Mysore, and although he did not know it then, would continue serving the kingdom for the rest of his life. By the time of the 1881 Rendition, when the kingdom was returned to the stewardship of the Wadiyars, Iyer had caught the eye of Maharaja Chamarajendra X, who lost no time appointing him officer on special duty in the capital. Two years later, when the position of dewan fell vacant with the retirement of CV Rungacharlu, Seshadri Iyer was at hand to fill it.

The two decades that followed the transition of power to the maharaja were crucial not only to Mysore's self-esteem, but also to British (and Indian) perceptions of native administrations in general. It would take a brave man, and one with great moral conviction, to function unhindered under the intense gaze of political watchers on all sides, some of whom wanted desperately for the experiment to succeed and others who were convinced it would fail. Fortunately for Mysore, the man who presided over eighteen of those twenty years was just such a one.

The first decade of Seshadri Iyer's dewanship saw a great slew of progressive developments brought in by the maharaja, ably supported by Iyer. In 1894, at only thirty-one, Chamarajendra tragically succumbed to diphtheria in faraway Calcutta, and Iyer was forced to take charge. The heir to the Mysore throne, Nalvadi Krishnaraja, was only ten at the time, so a suitable regent would have to be found to rule in his place until he turned eighteen. Despite a complete lack of administrative experience, five children to take care of, and her own grief to deal with, Chamarajendra's twenty-six-year-old widow, Maharani Kempananjammanni Vani Vilas Sannidhana, stepped bravely into the breach. Part of her courage came from the knowledge that she could rely on the good dewan to make the right decisions for Mysore.

Over the next seven years, until Iyer's death in 1901, the duo functioned as a formidable team. With the support of the maharani, Iyer created the Chamarajendra Water Works in Hessarghatta to supply drinking water to Bangalore; managed the plague that swept through the kingdom in 1898 by decongesting the crowded Pettah and creating the new residential extensions of Basavanagudi and Malleswaram to accommodate the displaced; signed a contract with General Electric to build Asia's largest hydroelectric station (which now bears his name) at Shivanasamudra, and established the Victoria Hospital, now India's second-largest hospital.

When Iyer passed at the age of fifty-six, Viceroy Curzon wrote to the Resident of Mysore, Donald Robertson, recommending that the dewan's unstinting services be honoured with some kind of long-lasting tribute. A memorial hall and a commemorative bronze statue located in the city's most premier location, Cubbon Park, being considered most appropriate, a public subscription was set up, to which Mysoreans of every stripe contributed generously. British sculptor William Robert Colton (more about him on page 64), who had made quite a name for himself in both London and Paris, was commissioned to make the statue. In November 1913, the Memorial Hall and the statue were inaugurated by Viceroy Hardinge.

The hall was meant for public use, but since no one had explicitly defined who comprised the 'public' and what manner of 'use' it was meant to be put to, it was taken over, as is usual in such cases, by a small and elite group of citizens for use as a private club. That kind of mischief was soon quashed by Sir M Visvesvaraya, the new dewan of Mysore, who ordered that a public library be started there forthwith.

Since 1986, that library has functioned as the State Central Library of Karnataka. In 2017, after a short closure for a much-needed renovation, the high-ceilinged, light-filled, apsidal space reopened to the public, looking better than ever before. Its massive collection of both rare and popular books, including close to a thousand in Braille,

The bronze statue of Kumarapuram Seshadri Iyer shows the dewan wearing the many awards and honours he had received, including the Knight Commander of the Most Exalted Order of the Star of India. Behind him is the memorial hall that bears his name.

apart from extensive documentary and digital archives, all accessible to any member of the public for free, is a most fitting tribute to a man who was at once socialist and capitalist, traditionalist and modernist, deeply religious and profoundly secular. A century after it first threw open its doors, the Seshadri Iyer Hall continues to welcome hundreds of visitors each day who value, above all, the inclusive serenity of both the hushed spaces inside and the verdant ones outside.

THE KING
The Wadiyar Who Raised the Bar

> *There is probably no state in India where the ruler and the ruled are on more satisfactory terms, or in which the great principle, that government should be for the happiness of the governed, receives a greater measure of practical recognition.*
>
> —Lord Lansdowne, Viceroy of India, speaking of Maharaja Chamarajendra Wadiyar X in 1892, as quoted in *History of Mysore* by Mark Wilks, edited by Murray Hammick, 1932

IF YOU FAVOUR THE SIDDALINGAIAH CIRCLE ENTRANCE (MORE commonly referred to as the Coffee Day Square entrance or the UB City entrance) that leads from Vittal Mallya Road into Cubbon Park, you will encounter the maharaja about 350 m of the way in, standing in his own little enclosure, encircled by potted blooms lovingly placed there in every season by the gardeners of the Horticulture Department. On days when the fountain installed directly opposite his statue is playing, you may have to look a little harder before you spot him.

Even though it was during his reign that Cubbon Park came into being, Chamarajendra was the last to get his spot there. That happened in 1927, as part of the silver jubilee celebrations of his son Nalvadi Krishnaraja. A bit of a shame, that, considering that it was Chamarajendra who set the precedent for Mysore being considered a model princely state for the next several decades, all the way until the monarchy itself was dismantled and India emerged as a republic.

A wonderful amalgam of the care and mentorship of the European guardians who oversaw his education, and the deep, strong roots of his ancestors, Chamarajendra Wadiyar X was as comfortable being a virtuoso Carnatic violinist as he was advocating for and formally establishing English-medium education for both boys and girls throughout the state. His reign was all too brief, but he managed to pack a lot into it and leave a considerable legacy. In Mysore, he made a gift of his private menagerie to the people of his kingdom, in the form of the Mysore Zoo (more correctly, the Chamarajendra Zoological Gardens). In Bangalore, he initiated the raising, in Lalbagh, of the iconic Glass House, so enamoured was he of the Crystal Palace in London's Hyde Park.

Perhaps his most revolutionary move, however, was instituting, in the very year he became king, the Representative Assembly of Mysore Kingdom. No other Indian princely state had a democratic, legislative institution at the time, and for a king to voluntarily choose to create one was a complete aberration. Happily for Mysore, the thread of his liberal imagination was picked up by his successors.

In 1907, his son, Nalvadi, would add a Legislative Council, a 'house of elders', to expand that assembly and make it bicameral. Nalvadi's nephew and heir,

Chamaraja Wadiyar X died very young, at age thirty-three, which makes this painting of him in happier times, surrounded by his five children, very special.

Jayachamarajendra, who had ruled for less than seven years when India got Independence, would become the first of the 565 'native princes' to sign the Instrument of Accession in August 1947, declaring graciously, '…the rule of the maharajas has indeed fulfilled its purpose, the purpose of making the people fit to rule themselves.'

In a roundabout way, Chamarajendra was also responsible for bringing the Indian Institute of Science to Bangalore. In 1892, urged by his dewan Seshadri Iyer, the king had made a generous gift of land and provided royal subsidies to Bombay industrialist Jamsetji Tata for the setting up of a silk farm in Bangalore. In 1893, he sponsored Swami Vivekananda's pathbreaking voyage to America, to speak at the Chicago Parliament of Religions. As luck would have it, these two men ended up travelling on the same ship. During their long conversations on deck, Jamsetji realized that the Swami's spiritual philosophy was also a most practical one. 'How wonderful it would be,' the Swami once exclaimed to Tata, 'if we could combine the scientific and technological achievements of the West with India's asceticism and humanism!'

Inspired, Jamsetji began to think of a project that would bring Vivekananda's vision to life, and zeroed in on education, specifically the vacuum that existed in India where institutes of higher education in science were concerned. Years later, having set aside several of his buildings and landed properties to create an endowment for his proposed scientific institute, Jamsetji met and discussed the project with his old friend Seshadri Iyer.

Chamarajendra had been dead four years by then, but a gung-ho Iyer recommended the project to his widow, the regent queen Vani Vilas Sannidhana, who unhesitatingly promised any support the Institute might need, on the condition that it be located in Bangalore. In 1909, although all three main players in the drama—Iyer, Swami Vivekananda and Jamsetji—were no longer around, their shared vision came to fruition in the shape of the Tata Institute (now the Indian Institute of Science) in Malleswaram, on 371 acres of land contributed by Chamarajendra's son, Krishnaraja.

And it was the king who came last to Cubbon Park who had kickstarted it all.

*

If Chamarajendra was special, so is his statue. Of all the ones in Cubbon Park, his is the only one not executed by a foreign sculptor. The Indian maestro responsible was Ganpatrao Mhatre, whose student work at the JJ School of Art had made him the toast of Bombay's art world in 1895. With nationalist feeling running high, wealthy Indian art-lovers, especially among the Parsi community, began to patronize Mhatre over European artists, and a host of commissions followed, including one of Queen Victoria for Kolhapur State, which made him the first Indian to be so commissioned.

Mhatre may never have been involved with Chamarajendra's statue if Robert Colton, the Wadiyars' favourite sculptor—he had executed the statue of Seshadri Iyer in Cubbon Park, and the eight snarling bronze tigers that no visitor to the Mysore Palace can miss—hadn't slipped up quite so badly on a different statue of Chamarajendra that he had been commissioned to make. When that sculpture arrived from London in 1918, the queen was most disapproving—the face of the statue, she complained, bore little resemblance to her late husband's. In a hush-hush intervention that was Mysore's worst-kept secret, Maharaja Nalvadi Krishnaraja invited Mhatre to create a new head for the statue. Mhatre complied, and swapping the new head with the original, hid the join behind a marble necklace. Today, the hybrid Colton-Mhatre creation graces one of Mysore's most prominent roundabouts, the Chamaraja Circle.

Naturally, when a new statue of his father had to be created for Cubbon Park in the lead up to his own silver-jubilee celebrations in 1927, Nalvadi turned to his new favourite. And Mhatre delivered. His sweet-faced Chamarajendra, captured in marble exactly as the king looked when he was cut down in the prime of his youth, stands at what is almost the exact centre of a Park that itself once lay at the intersection of two worlds.

Roopa Pai

The only one of the five statues in Cubbon Park executed by an Indian sculptor, this is also the last statue to have been added in a century and a half of the Park's existence.

The Enrichers

IN SOME WAYS, THE NUMBER OF EXPERTS, ACROSS A VARIETY of fields, that were drawn to Cubbon Park in the first hundred years of its existence borders on the surreal. After all, unlike Lalbagh, which started life as a sultan's pleasure garden and went on to be coddled and cared for by the world's top botanists, Cubbon Park has always been a people's park, a public commons, created not so much for its own sake as to enhance the status of the building it surrounded.

And yet, it is not Lalbagh but Cubbon Park that has been watched over by an empress for more than a hundred years of its existence. It was to the tennis courts at the latter that Surgeon Major Ronald Ross, who discovered the vector that carried the malaria bug during his time in India, regularly went to play a set or two in the last years of the 19th century. And it was along Cubbon Park's periphery that the acclaimed wildlife author, conservationist and hunter, the Scotsman Kenneth Anderson, lived in the 20th.

A different set of luminaries had a deeper engagement with the Park, each contributing something unique and precious to the space. Their names and stories are not as well-known as some of the others', but each enriched the Park in his or her own way, charging it with their vast talent, intelligence and large-heartedness.

THE CURATOR
Dr Edward Balfour and His Dazzling House of Fun

If you are driving north on Kasturba Road along the eastern edge of Cubbon Park, it is difficult to miss the glorious neoclassical building, arresting in (what else but) Pompeian red, that rises out of the ground to your left.

Against a monsoon-y Bangalore sky, the neoclassical elegance of the Government Museum contrasts sharply, but not jarringly, with the soaring chrome and glass of the UB City Tower.

Very few Bangaloreans, however, have ever set foot inside it. Quite a comedown for an establishment that, in the early 20th century, was famous far and wide as the Tamashe Bungalow, or the House of Fun, and attracted as many as 4,00,000 visitors annually. Today it is known—and only by the really, really curious—by the far tamer moniker of Government Museum.

Although the idea of a museum was fairly well established in Europe by the 18th century, it wasn't until 1850 that south India's first museum was founded in Madras. That museum, and the museum in Bangalore that followed in 1865, were created of the vision and labours of one remarkable man—the Scottish surgeon, orientalist, collector and environmentalist Edward Balfour.

Born in 1813, Balfour came from a family that had long served in India. His father was part of the East India Company marine service, and one of his maternal uncles, Joseph Hume, had been commissioned as a surgeon to an army regiment here before returning to England and beginning a full-fledged political career as an MP (one of Hume's sons, Allan Octavian Hume, would join the Indian Civil Service, and eventually found the Indian National Congress).

In the course of a fascinating life, Balfour would wear several hats. For one, he was a self-taught environmentalist, writing, as far back as 1849, original papers on climate change and the links between water and forest cover.

These papers, among others, led to the establishment of the Madras Forest Department in 1851, with the conservation of forest wealth as its main brief. As a medical man, his innate curiosity led him to become quite the public health expert—he was often called in to advice on choosing cantonment locations that would ensure good health for the troops. Recognizing the role of women in public health, he personally translated the book *Outlines of Midwifery* into Urdu, and paid from his own pocket for the Kannada, Tamil and Telugu translations.

One of Balfour's other great interests was collecting and classifying. In 1850, he founded the Government Central Museum in Madras, inviting members of the public to send in potential exhibits ('We accept everything!') and assuring them that the museum would pay for the postage and shipping. Since most of the museum's collection had been donated by the people themselves, there was no entrance fee. To encourage women, who were often in purdah, to visit, one day a week was set aside exclusively for them.

In time, Balfour, who was a great one for collating and analyzing data, realized that it was the museum's live exhibits—an orangutan once, a tiger cub another time—that drew the maximum visitors. That sparked an idea, and in 1855, the tireless man set up the country's first public zoo, the Madras Zoological Gardens.

When Balfour was transferred to Bangalore in the early 1860s, he found his reputation had preceded him. The then Commissioner of Mysore, Lewin Bowring, accepted with alacrity his suggestion that a museum be set up in Bangalore as well. In 1865, the second museum in south India, curated by Balfour himself, was set up in the premises of the Cantonment Jail (today the Good Shepherd Convent on Museum Road—see why the road is called that?).

A decade or so later, with the museum having outgrown its premises, it was decided to create an exclusive building for it. As always, it fell to Chief Engineer Richard Sankey to pick a location and come up with a design. With no hesitation, Sankey zeroed in on the eastern end of Cubbon Park's so-called Central Avenue, which had the Attara Kacheri at its western end. Keeping architectural integrity in mind, he designed the museum building in the same neoclassical style as the Kacheri. In 1877, the Mysore Government Museum moved to its posh new premises.

Today, a century and a half after it was first founded, Balfour's House of Fun is a desolate, deserted place, whose echoing halls feature dusty exhibits and incomplete or entirely missing signage. Despite containing such treasures in its collection as the Halmidi inscription, the oldest extant inscription in Kannada dated to the 5th century CE, and the Begur hero stone, which references, as far back as 890 CE, a town called Bengaluru, it fails to attract more than a hundred visitors a day.

The building that houses it, however, has not lost any of its charm. It also forms a great entranceway into Cubbon

Park—walk through the museum and out the back and you will see Richard Sankey's vision laid out before you. Follow the straight line of the Park's central east-west axis with your eyes and you will see a Grecian urn from Sankey's private collection, the statue of Mark Cubbon, the cast-iron bandstand from the 1920s, the original front entrance of the Attara Kacheri, and beyond and above it, if you squint hard, the gleaming Lion Capital at the top of the Vidhana

A late 19th-century picture of Cubbon Park's so-called Central Avenue. Today, Mark Cubbon and the bandstand stand between Sankey's urn and the Attara Kacheri.

Soudha's grand dome. Mr Hanumanthaiah (see page 157) would not be amused, but from this angle, with the Soudha entirely eclipsed by the Kacheri, it is yesterday once more at the Park.

THE HORTICULTURIST
Gustav Krumbiegel and the Royal Cubbon Park Swap

If you lived in Bengaluru/Bangalore in the years between 1906, when the statue of Queen Victoria was unveiled, and 1910, you might have felt some pity at the queen's magnificent isolation. Standing on top of her pedestal and looking down the city's main promenade towards St Mark's Church and Parade Ground, she was severely alone—even the few trees of Cubbon Park were quite a distance away behind her, and Sir Mark's statue well beyond them.

The 'bareness of the situation' annoyed the fine aesthetic sensibilities of forty-three-year-old Gustav Hermann Krumbiegel, the genius German horticulturist, architect and town planner who had just been brought in by the maharaja as his Superintendent of Government Gardens in 1907. By this time, Krumbiegel, who had worked in India since 1893 as a horticulturist at the royal gardens of Baroda, had made quite a name for himself. It had taken some wooing by Nalvadi Krishnaraja to bring him to Mysore, but now that he was here, he was a man in a hurry. Although Lalbagh was his main responsibility and passion, Krumbiegel also had the charge of Cubbon Park, and the statue was one of the first things that caught his attention. (You can read more about Krumbiegel's work in the books *Whatever He Touched, He Adorned* by Suresh Jayaram, and *Lalbagh: Sultan's Garden to Public Park* by VR Thiruvady.)

Eager to landscape the area around the statue to give it the grace and majesty it deserved, Krumbiegel found an unexpected obstacle quite literally in his path—a little police station situated close to the statue. No matter, the offending thing would simply have to be moved elsewhere. But when he petitioned the maharaja for permission, it turned out there was the small matter of jurisdiction. While the queen's statue and the rest of Cubbon Park lay within the maharaja's Bengaluru, the police station itself lay within the British Cantonment.

So Krumbiegel petitioned the British Resident Albert Williams with his problem. Williams had no objection to the police station being moved; his problem was where to move it to. Everyone agreed that the most convenient spot lay a little distance south of the statue, but that would mean encroaching on Park territory, and no one, not the dewan of Mysore VP Madhava Rao, not Krumbiegel, not even Albert Williams, wanted that. Other potential sites close by were considered, but none of them came through; regrettably, a part of the Park would have to be sacrificed.

A great many negotiations over the exact size of the parcel of land required followed, along with much hand-wringing on the dewan's part and reassurances from the resident about the care that would be taken to maintain the

Park's appearance. In 1909, to Krumbiegel's relief, the swap was finalized—793 sq m of the Park to be exchanged for 847 sq m of the Cantonment. The boundaries of City and Cantonment were redrawn, and Krumbiegel was finally free to add the ornamental railings around the statue, and all the flowering shrubs he wished to.

A year later, the new police station came up to the south of the queen's statue in the Cantonment. It stands there still on Kasturba Road, bearing the legends: '1910' and 'Police Station'—a silent and historic testimony to the very first, if very reluctant, encroachment of Cubbon Park.

An amusing take on the goings-on in the historic Cubbon Park Police Station in the '70s, by the brilliant Paul Fernandes, Bangalore's beloved visual chronicler. His Richards Town studio, aPaulogy, also serves as gallery and store.

THE ARCHITECT
Otto Koenigsberger and the 'Green' Bal Bhavan

What possible connection could the Jawahar Bal Bhavan, a space synonymous with Cubbon Park and carefree childhood to so many Bangaloreans, have with a German Jew fleeing Nazi persecution in World War II? As it turns out, a whole lot. Here's the short version of the story.

In 1933, Sir CV Raman, who had won the Nobel Prize for Physics three years earlier, moved to Bangalore to become the first Indian director of the Indian Institute of Science (IISc). Eager to set up a world-class Department of Physics there, he got to work finding and wooing world-class physicists. At the time, with Germany having just elected the anti-Semitic Nazi Party into power, many German Jews, among them talented scientists, had fled their country for safer shores, particularly the UK. One such was the physicist Max Born, who would win the Nobel Prize for Physics in 1954.

In 1935, Raman wrote to Born, offering him the position of visiting Reader in Theoretical Physics at IISc. Born accepted, and arrived with his wife to a beautiful bungalow on the IISc campus. Weeks later, when the dewan of Mysore, Mirza Ismail, with whom Born had developed a warm friendship, asked the physicist if he knew of any talented architects who could work for Mysore, Born recommended his own nephew, Otto Koenigsberger. In 1939, the thirty-one-year-old Koenigsberger arrived in

Bangalore from Cairo, where he had been employed as an archaeological researcher, to take over as chief architect and planner to Mysore state.

The fact that Koenigsberger worked in Mysore through World War II meant that he had to make do with very limited access to building materials and resources, especially cement, steel and glass. He also had to deal with the resentment of the Indian engineers of the Mysore PWD, who did not see why they should kowtow to a young German who wasn't even a 'real' engineer in the first place.

Perhaps his biggest challenge, however, was that his tastes in architecture were radically different from Mirza Ismail's. While Mirza saw Bangalore as a city of grand, monumental buildings—domes, clock towers, et al, all exhibiting perfect axial symmetry—that showcased the glory of Mysore, Koenigsberger was excited by the inexpensive, climate-responsive architecture of traditional homes in Mysore state, which used local materials in combination with architectural elements like chajjas and jalis. Unfortunately for Otto, Mirza's tastes were shared by most wealthy Mysoreans, who were the chief financiers of public buildings.

There was worse to come. The British Resident at the Mysore court disapproved mightily of the maharaja employing Germans in his administration when there was a war on. Koenigsberger and other 'Mysore Germans', like the kingdom's Chief Horticulturist Gustav Krumbiegel (who, not being Jewish, was considered a greater enemy of the state), were forced to spend time in internment camps, under constant threat of being deported. Fortunately, most of them survived the experience without too much heartache, chiefly because the maharaja was so firmly on their side, constantly advocating with the resident for their comfort and release.

In 1948, Koenigsberger was handpicked by Prime Minister Nehru to be the first Director of Housing for the government of India, and urged to use his talent for inexpensive innovation to create low-cost housing

Otto Koenigsberger with India's first prime minister, Jawaharlal Nehru. Impressed with his low-cost, sustainable approach to architecture, Nehru invited the architect, himself a refugee from Nazi Germany, to design houses for the refugees of Partition.

settlements for the millions displaced by Partition. Otto's marvellous idea of pre-fab aerated-concrete wall panels that were to be assembled onsite unfortunately failed in practice. Following the storm in the Indian Parliament, he resigned from his post and returned to England in 1951. Welcomed by the Architectural Association as the head of the department of Development and Tropical Studies, he pioneered a whole new field of study—Climatic Design—based on his experiences in India. His book *Manual of Tropical Housing and Building: Climatic Design* is to this day part of the canon for students of architecture across the world.

What does all this of this have to do with Bal Bhavan? To most old Bangaloreans, 'Bal Bhavan' refers not just to the quaintly shaped auditorium that holds such precious childhood memories of movie screenings and plays and concerts, but also to the extensive 12.5-acre grounds around it, that have, for decades, provided the city's children with access to swings and jungle gyms, picnic gazebos and fun summer camps, popcorn kiosks and cotton candy vendors, and the beloved toy train, the Putani Express.

It is only the auditorium that is relevant to this story, however. Originally styled 'Victory Hall' and meant as a memorial building to commemorate the Allied victory in World War II, it was designed, like several buildings on the IISc campus and elsewhere in Bangalore, by our friend Koenigsberger.

Minimalist and modish, Koenigsberger's Victory Hall still holds its own against the modern office building behind it.

A triumph of sustainable construction, and climate-responsive enough to never need air-conditioning, Victory Hall is a remarkable building. In the absence of cement and steel, Otto used granite masonry for load-bearing walls. For lobby and veranda roofs, he fashioned lightweight concrete vault shells whose shape mirrored the eaves of south Indian temples. In place of expensive RCC beams, he used bowstring girders to span the roof of the main building. Striking because of its unusual shape—rounded, squat, and rooted to the earth rather than reaching for the skies—the hall brought to mind, as Otto meant it to, the 'softly moulded boulders' of the Deccan landscape.

Predictably, none of its wealthy patrons liked the look

of Victory Hall when it was finished in 1946. The real tragedy, however, lay elsewhere. Neither Krumbiegel—who was also often called in to design public buildings—nor Koenigsberger ever got credit for the structures they designed. Before Independence, giving the Germans credit was tantamount to treason; after, everyone simply forgot.

And that's the story of how, years and years before the term 'sustainable architecture' was even invented, a proto 'green architect' from faraway Germany bestowed one more in a long line of accidental benedictions on Cubbon Park.

THE PARROT
A Nepalese Queen's Pet Project

In 1926, on the recommendation of his venerable dewan Sir M Visvesvaraya, Nalvadi Krishnaraja Wadiyar joyously appointed Sir Mirza Ismail as the next Dewan of Mysore. The joy owed mainly to the fact that Mirza and Nalvadi had been the closest of friends for years, having first come together in the schoolroom as boys in short pants. Mirza had served as the maharaja's private secretary since 1905, and taken on many other administrative roles besides, but to have him serve the kingdom as dewan was a different pleasure altogether.

Mentored by Sir MV, one of whose dictums was 'Industrialize or perish!', Sir Mirza had his eye firmly on keeping Mysore in the fast lane—it was during his dewanship that the kingdom's rural electrification programme was initiated and factories to manufacture sugar, paper, cement, steel, fertilizer and electric bulbs were set up across the state. He was also instrumental in clearing all hurdles to the setting up of Hindustan Aircraft (now Aeronautics) Limited in Bangalore in 1940.

The dapper Sir Mirza (second from left) seen here with his friend, the Nobel Laureate Sir CV Raman (in the Mysore peta, or turban), and Nobel Laureate Max Born (second from right), who was then teaching at the Indian Institute of Science in Bangalore. It was Born's nephew, Otto Koenigsberger, who designed the Victory Hall in Cubbon Park (see page 75).

But Sir Mirza was also an aesthete. He believed it was 'obligatory for the administration' to create beautiful urban spaces that the poor, particularly, could enjoy at no expense. His fascination with fountains and gardens ensured that work on Mysore's Brindavan Gardens began the very year he took office. Working closely with 'the Maharaja's German gardener', the very talented landscapist, horticulturist and town planner Gustav Krumbiegel, the gardens, inspired by Mughal gardens, were designed as a charbagh. Laid out across three terraces and punctuated with pergolas, gazebos and the famous fountains, they were thrown open to an awe-stricken public in 1932.

It bothered Sir Mirza, though, that Bangalore did not have its own 'fairy fountain'. Sometime after the Brindavan Gardens was inaugurated, the dewan was approached by the Maharani of Bahjang (a principality in Nepal), who had made her home in Bangalore, with a rather unconventional request. Anxious about the future of her

The fairy fountain that a parrot made possible.

pet parrot should something happen to her, she asked if Sir Mirza could arrange for the bird to be taken care of in Lalbagh (where a few birds were kept at the time) in the event. She even pressed upon him a sum of 5,000 rupees to cover all expenses.

A startled Sir Mirza reassured her on the parrot's account, but requested that he be allowed to use the money for a public project that could be enjoyed by everyone. The maharani agreed. Of course, Sir Mirza knew exactly what project he would use it for, and exactly where it would be located. He immediately commissioned the construction of a fairy fountain opposite the statue of Chamarajendra Wadiyar in Cubbon Park.

Soon, funds began to run low, and he was forced to approach the maharani again, to ask for a further Rs 3,000, which she gladly dispensed. By the time the fountain was ready, however, the maharani had moved to Bombay for good, along with her parrot. Sadly, although she was delighted that her money had been put to such good use, neither the maharani, who passed away soon after, nor her parrot, of whose fate nothing is known, ever got to see the beautiful fountain they had gifted to the city.

People of the Park

The Last Fifty Years

The Lovers

IN WHICH THE PARK SPEAKS, THROUGH THE BIRDS AND THE BEES AND THE TREES

At the end of December, you arrive one morning to find that the silk cotton tree has started blooming. Far up above in the canopy, small orange flowers against the blue sky. Which means it's been a year since you first started visiting this tree. What a year it has been. And what a ritual this has been. The only constant that has grounded you through upheavals, shocks, surges of delight, joy, lightness, heaviness… and as always, an endless return to humility.

—Asha Mokashi, French translator and technical writer, writing about Cubbon Park in her blog, whiletheworldisgoingplaces.blogspot.com

I always loved this place. Trees here are so kind and welcoming. They fill you with positive thoughts. Very well kept and managed without letting Nature be an obvious pet of humans. Come here early in the morning, bathe yourself in the sun…

—Visitor to Bangalore Shraddha Bhowad, in her December 2019 review of Cubbon Park for tripadvisor.com

Vijay Thiruvady is more a Lalbagh man than a Cubbon Park one (this, as you will realize when you have spent enough time among Bangaloreans, is an important distinction). He is the author of a much-acclaimed book on Lalbagh, and for the last twenty years, has spent almost every weekend, and hundreds of weekdays, walking among the trees there—observing them, researching them, befriending them, enjoying them. In the last fifteen years, he has also told their stories to thousands of people of all ages from across the world, who listen, rapt, to a most unusual raconteur, who seamlessly brings together in his tree stories geology and history, engineering and botany, architecture and art, culture and philosophy.

The granite outcrops in the Park are a constant and visible reminder of Bangalore's topography.

Where did Vijay's long and eclectic career—he pursued his academic interests at St Stephen's, Delhi, and the School of Architecture in Ahmedabad, farmed his family's ancestral land in Tamil Nadu for many years as a young man, and consulted with some of the world's best-known engineering companies—leave him time for trees? Where does that abiding love for nature come from? 'I am very lucky to have grown up in the home of my maternal grandfather*,' he says. 'The bungalow was set in the middle of a three-acre garden in Lutyens' Delhi, and I had the run of the place. As a teenager, I got to accompany some of the top people in ornithology in the capital—Khushwant Singh, for instance—on birding expeditions, and read books on Delhi birds by fellow citizens like the British High Commissioner Malcolm McDonald, who was a neighbour. That was where it all began.'

It came to fruition, though, when he went to live with his paternal grandmother and farm his family's land. 'It was the best time of my life. I have never felt so fulfilled or so entirely self-reliant—even the cloth for the khaddar shirts I wore had been woven out of the cotton I grew. There is a great joy in coaxing things out of the earth, a special bond is built with the land.' When he retired, he found the time

---

*Vijay's grandfather was the scientist Sir KS Krishnan, the founder-director of the National Physical Laboratories, and co-discoverer, with Nobel laureate Sir CV Raman, of the 'Raman Effect'.

to indulge that long-nourished love full-time, by bonding with the trees of Lalbagh.

A few years ago, fortunately for all of us, Vijay also began telling Cubbon Park stories. What, in his opinion, makes the Park special? 'It is the best introduction to the British in Bangalore,' shrugs the octogenarian. 'In the Park, and around it, is every institution the British believed was important for human well-being—lawns (a most un-Indian concept), carriageways (the path that leads into the Park from the Hudson Circle entrance is landscaped very much like those leading up to manor houses in England), a museum, a library, a bandstand (where military bands, of a Sunday afternoon, played their fifes and drums), a brewery (now defunct), a gentleman's club (now called the Bangalore Club), a horse racing track, a golf course, and the Park itself. There was also the annual Bangalore Hunt, whose route went right past the Park towards the wilds of Varthur, when riders and their hounds hunted down jackals. Given that Cubbon Park was and continues to be in the centre of the city, the impact of these institutions on the city's culture has been profound.'

That's a great insight. Despite all the changes the city has been through in the 152 years of the Park's existence, and the hundreds of thousands of immigrants that have poured into it in the last couple of decades, Bangalore continues to be a reading city which loves its gardens, its museums—the city has close to twenty private museums—its golf, its dogs and its beer.

A poem by Karnataka's pre-eminent poet laureate, Kuvempu, graces a sign at the High Court entrance to the Park.

God and flowers

O Poojari,
If you didn't behead these gentle blossoms
Haul them into the black darkness of the sanctum
And offer them as a sacrifice to that stone,
Would God not be content?
If you left them, resplendent, on the plant,
Would the worship be incomplete?
Could the Earth remain blessed
If you plucked out Shiva's very eyes
From his radiant face?
Let them be, man! Why destroy
That which you could never create?

(Translation by the author)

The Park itself has changed, though. What Richard Sankey had envisaged as rolling lawns punctuated by tree-shaded nooks is now a densely wooded area with only a few wide-open spaces. 'Over the years, the tree-planting here has been rather enthusiastic,' agrees Vijay. 'Many have been planted haphazardly, sometimes not leaving enough room between saplings. Looking for the sun, trees have grown taller than usual, which makes it difficult for visitors to enjoy the flowering trees because their canopies are so high up. But a park, by definition, is a large public garden used for recreation, and that is exactly how Bangaloreans see and use Cubbon Park. In that sense, it has stayed true to Sankey's vision for it.'

Many of the saplings that were originally planted in the Park came from Lalbagh, by then a well-established British botanical garden where non-native plants and trees were acclimatized. 'Cubbon Park is full of exotics, which do not support as much local fauna as native trees,' says S 'Karthik' Karthikeyan, insect-watcher, photographer and naturalist of over thirty years standing. Karthik was talking about 'urban wildlife' way back in the '90s, when few people were familiar with the phrase. 'But there is still a sizeable population of insects and reptiles and birds.' He should know. In 1998, when the whole city came together to protest the denotification of 32 acres of the Park, Karthik was part of a group of bird-watchers, zoologists and environmentalists who did an informal census of the flora and fauna in the park. They identified 110 species of medicinal plants, some forty species of butterflies, and over sixty-three species of birds.

In the mid-80s, then a teenager, Karthik volunteered with the World Wildlife Fund (WWF) India as an instructor in several of their nature camps for schoolchildren. In 1992, as a full-fledged employee, he got even more involved with nature walks and talks for both students and teachers. He even wrote a little book for WWF called *Fauna of Bangalore: Vertebrates and Butterflies of Bangalore* which listed about 650 different species. It was the first checklist of its kind in India, and still serves as baseline data for the city's fauna. 'The book was a direct fallout of talking to students about the creatures they see around them,' he says. 'I realized that very few people see as much wildlife as I do, because no one sees bugs and beetles and grasshoppers as "wildlife".'

In later years, as chief naturalist with Jungle Lodges and Resorts, Karthik continued to educate, this time training the guides who accompanied tourists on safaris into Karnataka's forest reserves. He also started blogging about all creatures great and small (mostly small), and the city's flowering trees, at www.wildwanderer.com; new posts continue to appear there regularly. In the past few years, he has regularly run nature walks in Cubbon Park for organizations like INTACH. 'Not many of us realize it, but Bangalore is actually at the exact centre of the southern peninsula, between the eastern and western ghats. That makes places like Cubbon Park the perfect staging area for migratory birds. The Park also supports swarms of butterflies as they move across the peninsula from one range to the other—they're a jaw-dropping sight.'

That's not the only reason he believes the Park is special. 'Cubbon Park is a very, very important lung space. Sure, an urban park is fundamentally meant for people to enjoy, and it is a "created" green space, so its design is going to be human-centric—there are going to be "pretty" plants and trees, there is going to be some concrete—and that's fine. But it is still a fantastic and essential repository of urban biodiversity. That makes it very precious.'

Prem Koshy, musician, actor, and the genial proprietor of the iconic eighty-year-old Koshy's restaurant, located literally a stone's throw away from Queen Vic, knows better than most about the Park's biodiversity. As part of the advisory board of People For Animals (PFA) Bangalore and a member of their React and Rescue (R&R) Team for decades, he has been called out countless times to rescue and rehabilitate snakes—rat snakes, cobras, arboreal bronzebacks, sawscaled vipers, Russell's vipers—birds of all kinds, and once, even a pangolin, from the Park.

It was from his maternal grandfather, an animal healer who was, Prem swears, the wisest man he has ever known, that he picked up his own animal-whisperer skills. But everyone in the family was a conservationist. 'My paternal grandfather, who founded Koshy's, walked me through Cubbon Park the day after I was born,' laughs Prem. 'And Bangalore's first R&R centre was my home—whenever anyone rescued an animal, they just brought it home.'

Prem believes that no other city, in India or elsewhere, has the diversity, numbers and safe spaces for urban wildlife that Bangalore does, with Cubbon Park as its touchstone. His connection with the Park borders on the spiritual. 'In the Park, the earth speaks to you. Come, it says, jump on me, sit on me, roll around in my leaves. It doesn't do that in Lalbagh, the land has a different personality there, distant, snooty. Every space is imbued with the energy of the people who visit it.'

One of the reasons people visit Cubbon Park is to be part of a guided walk. But what is it that brings people who lead those walks, like Vijay and Karthik, there? 'It was only at the age of sixty-five, when I started leading walks for Arun Pai's Bangalore Walks, that I discovered that I was a gregarious person who loved being with people and sharing what I knew,' smiles Vijay. 'The innocent questions people ask me about trees have often confounded me and sent me scurrying down tortuous rabbit holes, looking for answers. That process, of igniting curiosity about the natural world in others, keeps my own sense of wonder alive.' (Vijay's tree stories are now available for free viewing on YouTube—look for the Treespotting series on the Bangalore Walks channel.)

Karthik is impelled by a more urgent need, but he uses much the same language to describe it. 'Nature education for the young, that's what gets me going. Travelling to a nature reserve to see large animals is wonderful, but how often can any of us do it? Come to Cubbon Park for a couple of hours instead, and, on a good day, I can show you a miniature universe within a 100-m walk. Once that portal has been unlocked, a child will look at every green space—her own backyard, even—with curiosity and wonder. A nature-lover has been created.'

IN WHICH THE PARK BEWITCHES THE CITY WITH MUSIC UNDER THE STARS

> *In the seventies*, an experiment called 'Music Strip' sprouted in Cubbon Park, like grass after rain. One microphone, a battery-operated amplifier and a speaker. A mixed audience, united only by the music, listened unharassed from the fringes of the petromax light. In semi-darkness, with snacks, drinks and 'joints'. We used to be a free society.*
>
> —Peter Colaco, in *Bangalore: A Century of Tales from City and Cantonment*

---

*Peter was off by a decade. The Music Strip was an '80s phenomenon.

> *The freakishly informal set-up was just perfect. It was sort of a neutral place in between City and Cantonment, so there were no cultural problems.*
>
> —Sunbeam 'Boom Shankar' Motha, the founding force behind the Cubbon Park Music Strip, speaking about it in the now-defunct blog onmusicbeat

GOPAL NAVALE WAS IN HIS EARLY TWENTIES WHEN HE HEARD, over the grapevine, about a weekly 'jam' that had begun to happen in Cubbon Park on Saturday evenings. 'I grew up in Seshadripuram in an orthodox family,' he recalls. 'My sisters dutifully learnt Carnatic music, since girls were reckoned to be keepers of the tradition. With my convent school background, I eventually picked up a guitar.' But the neighbourhood guitar teacher only taught chords to Bollywood songs, so over the '70s, Gopal taught himself to play the rock 'n' roll songs he loved by listening keenly when they played on the radio.

The news of the weekly jam was, literally, music to his ears. The live music scene in Bangalore, which had gone underground during the Emergency years, had anyway been limited to Cantonment cabarets like Three Aces, Boscos and Omar Khayyam, where Gopal would have never been allowed to go. But now it was all happening in familiar old Cubbon Park—what could be better?

The man behind the revolutionary concept of the Strip was a young maverick called Sunbeam Motha. In 1972, still eighteen, Beam had decided to travel the world instead of going to college. With only the money he had made off the sale of his high-end racing bike, the cycling champion hitchhiked 'from Fraser Town to Europe', spending a considerable time in Germany before returning home, his head bursting with new ideas, hippie culture, and music—street music, world music, jazz, fusion. Now keen to connect with the music of 'the other half', the Cantonment boy crossed the great divide and began to frequent the annual Ramanavami concerts of Carnatic and Hindustani music at the Fort High School in the erstwhile City.

In 1983, Bombay businessman Shorab Rubina brought the play *Dear Liar: A Comedy of Letters* starring Laura and Geoffrey Kendall to Bangalore for a show at the Chowdiah Memorial Hall. Instead of going the flyer route, Rubina wanted to try streetside busking as a promotional strategy. Beam was not a musician himself, but he counted several among his closest friends; he offered to help Rubina set it all up. The plan was to get the musicians to perform on the raised embankment on the Parade Ground side of MG Road, but the police commissioner denied Rubina permission, offering him instead a strip of green in Cubbon Park, between the statues of Victoria and Edward VII, to do as he pleased. With no fences in place yet, the strip gave directly on to the road—the promotion, and the play itself, were a great success.

Something about Beam's infectious enthusiasm and the

whole spirit of 'music in the Park' warmed Rubina's heart. Before he left, he handed over 5,000 rupees from the play's profits to Beam, and asked him to keep the music going on 'the Strip', with the condition that it be run solely by musicians, and always for free. Delighted, Beam lost no time in roping in his friends, musicians Peter Pires, Michael Furtado and Geoffrey Pope, and registering The Bangalore Music Strip Trust.

Paul Fernandes' ode to the Cubbon Park Music Strip. As a young man, Paul was often at the Strip, and remembers being utterly captivated by the atmosphere.

Thus began a never-before, never-again, three-year-long, free weekend festival that music-loving Bangaloreans who were young then remember as absolutely magical. At the Strip, original music took precedence over covers, and disco, all the rage across the world, was a bad word. 'There was no formal programme, no posters, no tickets, no newspaper ads, no radio announcements,' remembers Gopal. 'But come Sunday evening and a bunch of people from all over the city would gravitate towards the Strip, looking forward to some great music under the stars. Really, that's all it was.'

In the initial months, it was the city's older set of musicians who took the stage each weekend. At the time, the Strip was also an entirely acoustic experience, since there was no power source nearby. Keen to get some young blood into the mix, Beam dropped in on legendary Bangalore guitarist, Konarak Reddy, to ask him to be part of the Strip. Konarak wished Beam well, but declined to participate, since he only played electric. That was when a third friend, Venkatachalam, who happened to be around that day, suggested a hack. 'In those days, Ahuja—the sound solutions guys—used to make battery-run amplifiers for use in political rallies,' remembers Konarak. 'Chalam suggested hitching those up to car batteries and my speakers, and see what happened. We went out and hired the amps, and moved the "stage" a little deeper inside the Park, to where the rocks were, for better acoustics. I tried the whole contraption out with an electric guitar and a gadget called a Baseline, and it sounded amazing.' The electric Strip was born.

Each Sunday's fare was varied, a smorgasbord of

unexpected delights, as well-known and not-so-well-known musicians, both Indian and western, performed rehearsed and unrehearsed music. In time, the Strip moved to the lawns in front of the Cubbon Park Bandstand, where there was access to electricity. Occasionally, the Strip even went posh, setting up inside the Bal Bhavan's 'proper' 300-seater auditorium. As the legend spread, Max Mueller Bhavan (now the Goethe Institut) stepped in to help Beam buy batteries, amps, and a mic, and audiences and bands began to come in from Chennai, Kodaikanal and Goa, all eager to revel in the Strip's bohemian, everyone's-welcome vibe.

The vast majority of acts, however, remained homegrown. Before he became a celebrated poet, local boy Jeet Thayil was a punk rock musician at the Strip. He continues to play 'psychedelic grime' with his band, Still Dirty. Peter Isaac and his Chronic Blues Band were regulars, as were Siddhartha Patnaik and his reggae outfit Bharat Mata Nach Kud Baja, jazz diva Radha Thomas, and of course, Konarak Reddy.

'Peter lived on a farm in Hoskote,' recounts fanboy Navale, his excitement palpable even after all these years. 'He always performed in a lungi to show solidarity with farmers. Jeet was completely wild—at one of the bigger Strip events, which happened at the Bandstand, he decided, at the last minute, that his hastily put-together band would be called Dr Dong and the Wrinkled Scrotums. Rajeev Raja, who now lives and performs in Bombay, was so annoyed that he refused to go up on stage, insisting he wasn't going to be referred to as a wrinkled scrotum. Oh, and Konarak used to make and sell coin pizzas for five bucks each. I'm not sure where the power for the oven came from.'

'It was egg sandwiches, as I remember,' laughs Konarak, when questioned. 'But even if it was pizza, I lived so close to Cubbon Park, on St Mark's Road, that I just made the food at home and brought it with me. After the show ended at some point in the night, we'd hitch rides with friends to Nandi Hills, to continue the revelries there.'

Did anyone ever come by to break up the party? Cops, disapproving citizenry, self-styled guardians of the Park? 'Not at all. Bangalore was a gentler city then. As long as there was nothing criminal or violent going on, the cops were happy to leave people, even the lovers, alone. I remember there were these two Australian boys hitchhiking through Bangalore in the seventies. They'd busk on MG Road in the day and sleep in Cubbon Park at night. I don't recall them saying they felt unsafe or harassed.'

Konarak's wife, Kirtana Kumar, a well-known actor and director who runs Little Jasmine Theatre Project, a children's theatre company, and Theatre Lab, a theatre pedagogy programme for the youth, has great memories of singing at the Strip herself. She is convinced that the Strip owed a big part of its success to its location. 'Cubbon Park has always been a confluence,' she says. 'When I was growing up, my maternal grandparents lived on the City side, my other grandparents on the Cantonment side. The one place we all came together, where we all felt at home, was the Park, whether it was lunches at the Century Club or picnic teas on the lawns or a visit to the State Central Library on our birthdays.'

Even Cubbon Park could not stop the Strip from being shut down, however. In 1986, Beam and his co-founders got their marching orders from the local police. But a spark had been kindled, and would not be doused. The ones who carried the torch most passionately were Gopal

A poster for Freedom Jam 2016, designed by Siddhartha Patnaik, who, after his partner Gopal Navale moved out in 2008, continues to host the festival on Independence Day each year.

Navale, by then helming his own fusion band Esperanto, and Siddhartha Patnaik. In 1996, on the occasion of the fiftieth anniversary of Indian Independence, they launched Freedom Jam, an annual event that carried on the spirit of the '80s Strip by inviting musicians to perform for free and encouraging them to play original compositions. That went so well that the duo was emboldened to launch the monthly Sunday Jams, not at the Park but elsewhere in the city.

By the noughties, both Freedom Jam and Sunday Jam had become such hot properties that corporates, first UB, then Levi's, jumped in, begging for a piece of the action. In 2008, after putting together twelve Freedom Jams and a whopping 144 Sunday Jams, during which every Bangalore band, known and unknown, professional, amateur and college, had taken the stage, Gopal bowed out of the partnership to focus on his own musical career. In 2009, Sunbeam Motha passed away; he was only fifty-four.

The Sunday Jams ended, but Siddhartha continues to host the Freedom Jam—the most recent one, the 24th edition in 2019, featured internationally renowned double violin virtuoso L Shankar as part of an EDM Rock Music Extravaganza. As always, the artistes performed for free, the performance was not ticketed, and the music was as eclectic as they come.

Against all odds, some forty years after it first caught Bangalore's imagination, the spirit of the Strip lives on in the city, and in the rocks and grasses of the Park where it all began.

IN WHICH THE PARK TURNS EVERY COLOUR OF THE RAINBOW

> *Cubbon Park, especially the inner road between the Press Club and the High Court, has been a gay cruising area at least since the '60s, when I was a teenager. That stretch was referred to as Peacock Drive, and there was a lot of action after dark in the area around the boulders, especially inside the bamboo groves. The police came around sometimes, but they'd usually go away if you gave them two rupees. That was before Bangalore had any LGBT support groups.*
>
> —Patrick Wilson, designer, social activist and counsellor for HIV and LGBTQIA+ issues

> *How does a city contribute to personal growth? And if it does, can we say that geography determines sensitivity? Bangalore is known as a laidback city. Perhaps that explains some of the support the gay rights movement has received from different sources, including the media. Bangalore fosters the fight, however hesitant, for those who are considered different.*
>
> —Vinay Chandran, Executive Director, Swabhava Trust, an NGO that has worked with the city's LGBTQIA+ community since 1999, in *The Hindu*, 2011

ARVIND NARRAIN HAS SPENT A LOT OF HIS LIFE AROUND Cubbon Park. For one thing, he has always lived in the area. As a child, he was often to be found here on weekend mornings with his many cousins, who all lived around him, daredevil-cycling up the boulders. When he was in the eighth or ninth grade, he began running in the Park, a morning activity that he still enjoys thirty-five years on. In the late '80s, struggling with being different from his classmates at St Joseph's Boys' School, he drew strength from the headlines that occasionally appeared in the daily newspapers, about men being shooed out of Cubbon Park for indulging in 'illegal sexual activities'.

'They were without exception negative headlines,' remembers Arvind. 'But they transmuted into something powerful and positive in my head. I knew now that there were other people out there like me, that I wasn't alone. That was very good news indeed.'

In 1988, the country's first National Law University, a premier institute with the mission to pioneer legal education reforms and transform the Indian legal system, began operations in Bangalore as the National Law School of India University (NLSIU). Four years later, along with hundreds of India's brightest eighteen-year-olds who did not want to study medicine or engineering, Arvind sat for the tough entrance exam and made it through. The NLSIU campus was a radical space, where all kinds of contrarian views and ideologies found support and new recruits, but alternate sexualities was still an uncommon topic, so Arvind kept his thoughts to himself.

Law school turned Arvind into an activist, however. In 1996, after attending a seminar on The Child and the Law, he decided, along with his best friend, Sanjay Bavikatte, and a few others, to do something to rehabilitate the city's street children. Needless to say, one of the first places they looked was Cubbon Park—with no gates or fences, the Park used to be a refuge for all kinds of vagrants. Sure enough, they soon found a group of nine children, all under the age of fifteen, living entirely by their wits. Arvind and his friends began to spend a lot of time with the children, trying to understand what might be the best way to help them. When the children were suddenly hauled off to jail—they were going to be sent to a Remand Home, the idea of which they hated—Arvind not only got them released but also arranged for temporary shelter in the compound of his parents' house, before a more permanent home was found.

In his final year, bouncing off ideas with Bavikatte on building a CV that would get them a good shot at a Master's programme abroad, Arvind suggested they write a piece on gay rights. 'Sanjay looked straight at me and asked if I was gay,' remembers Arvind. 'I was so startled that I said yes without even thinking.' Stunned and sad that his friend had not even felt comfortable enough to come out to him in all those years, Bavikatte decided something revolutionary had to be done. 'Forget writing a piece,' he told Arvind. 'We are organizing a seminar.'

That was the genesis of Bangalore's very first gay rights seminar in September 1997. Organized over a weekend at the NLSIU campus, but without the blessings of the administration—the director, believing that there were other, more pressing, issues NLSIU would prefer to be associated with in the fiftieth year of India's Independence, agreed only to provide the space—it was a spectacular success. Beginning with the curtain-raisers and going on to the post-seminar analyses and editorials, it seemed Bangalore's newspapers talked about nothing else for a week. In the space of that week, queer issues came out of the closet and into the city's mainstream discourse for good.

'The run-up to the seminar changed everything,' recalls Arvind. 'In our hunt for suitable speakers, we got in touch with several queer support groups across the country that I had known nothing about until then. There was one—Good As You (GAY)—in our own city, that had been functioning for about three years then. And I had had no idea of its existence!'

Soon, Arvind had not only become part of GAY (hosted by eminent playwright Mahesh Dattani in his office space, GAY's mission was to get people together for 'something more constructive than a bitching session and less formal than a meeting') but also launched, along with both gay and lesbian groups and allies, a platform to discuss sexuality issues called Sabrang.

One fine Bangalore Sunday evening in 1998, four gay teenagers who were hanging out around a *butta* vendor's cart near the Press Club in the Park, minding their own business, got picked up and questioned for hours inside

Sangama all staff go to the Protest.

NO ENTRY FOR POOR AND COMMON PEOPLE TO CUBBON PARK AND LALBAGH

(ENTRY RESTRICTED TO ID CARD HOLDING ELITES ONLY)

The Government of Karnataka plans to make ID cards mandatory to enter Cubbon Park and Lalbagh, and that at a cost of Rs 200/person. This is the beginning of the state's encroachment of people's right to freely access public spaces. All sorts of reasons are being flung at the public, including security concerns, morality and misuse of parks by "unnecessary elements".

The manner in which the policy is formulated encourages the particular exclusion of access rights of the urban poor (especially from minorities), street and working children, elderly people, transgenders, migrant workers, labourers, street vendors, drivers of autorickshaws and taxis, differently abled, families with children, etc. The idea of having to carry an ID merely to access these two parks, fundamentally distances them from their unfettered and constitutionally protected Right to Use Public Spaces. This policy also promotes discriminatory access to public spaces as it privileges 'regular walkers' and thus negates the very concept of parks as public commons. Simply stated this draconian policy encroaches our very fundamental Right to Live a Healthy Life based on dignified and unfettered access to public spaces.

Join the Protest against this fundamental encroachment of Our Right to Access all Public Commons

COME JOIN THIS JUST PROTEST WITH FAMILIES, COLLEAGUES, FRIENDS, NEIGHBOURS

Queen's Statue, Cubbon park, Monday, 30th November, 4.00 pm

Protest initiated by Environment Support Group, CIEDS, Vimochana, Dalit Sangharsh Samiti- Samyojaka - (Bangalore Dist.), Sanmathi, Alternative Law Forum, Sangama and Stree Jagrithi Samithi

For more details contact: Environment Support Group,1572, Outer Ring Road, Banshankari 2nd stage, Bangalore-560070 Tel:-91-80-26713559-60 Email:esg@esgindia.org, bhargavi@esgindia.org Website: www.esgindia.org

A 2009 poster calling for public support in a protest against a proposal by the government concerning entry into Cubbon Park. The protest was initiated by several organizations, including ALF and Sangama, a human rights organization that works with sexual minorities and other marginalized groups, particularly from poor and non-English speaking backgrounds.

File 42, Sangama Organisational, Sangama Collection. QAMRA Archival Project at NLSIU. Accessed on: 27/06/2022 a police vehicle. Furious, Sabrang launched a leafletting campaign in Cubbon Park to protest the police harassment of gay people. The leaflet included Sabrang's contact details for the benefit of anyone in a similar situation, and demanded the repeal of Section 377 of the IPC, well before the official public interest litigation was filed in the Delhi High Court by the Naz Foundation in 2001. The campaign worked—it got a lot of press attention (several Sabrang allies were influential members of the press) and the police laid off, at least temporarily.

Two years later, Arvind co-founded the Alternative Law Forum (ALF), a collective of lawyers committed to a practice of law that would respond to issues of social and economic justice, particularly where it involved marginalized groups. He was also part of the team of lawyers that challenged Section 377, right from the hearing in the Delhi High Court in 2008 and the overturn of the section in 2009, to the final triumph of the Supreme Court ruling in 2018, which declared that the section was unconstitutional, thus finally and forever decriminalizing homosexuality in India. In January 2022, his explosive book *India's Undeclared Emergency* was launched to rave reviews.

Through all of it, however, Arvind has returned regularly to Cubbon Park. In 2008, he co-founded the GRAB—Gay Running And Breakfast—Club, which runs in the Park every Sunday before heading out to the Airlines Hotel for breakfast. 'The current western stereotype of gay men is that of people who are obsessed with working out, which is entirely contrary to the stereotype when I was growing up, of gay boys being completely uninterested in testosterone-fuelled sport,' he laughs. 'Like so many other stereotypes, both are true. That's why, these days, the annual Rainbow Run in Cubbon Park offers both a 3-km walk and a 5-km run, to bring more people out. There is also a queer-friendly yoga group that meets there on Sunday mornings.'

Part of the reason that Arvind's life has revolved around the Park is that his great-grandfather, the philanthropist Rai Bahadur Arcot Narrainsawmy Mudaliar, was the chief contractor on the Attara Kacheri building project under Richard Sankey. The Rai Bahadur owned large properties close by, parts of which have now passed on to his descendants. But what is it about the Park, in his opinion, that has also made it the place of choice for the LGBTQIA+ community to gather? 'It is a non-judgmental space,' shrugs Arvind, 'and an open space, both literally and figuratively. Unlike the city's streets, which are often chaotic, there's no need to jostle here, even metaphorically speaking. There's plenty of room for everyone.'

And Peacock Drive? Is it still a thing? Arvind is not sure. With the online world offering more opportunities to meet like-minded people than anyone can handle, there is no longer any need to slink around dark alleys after sundown, trying to find someone. In addition, Bangalore is home to dozens of global IT majors, whose diversity regulations ensure that there is a formal acceptance of the community in the workplace. More importantly, a large number of working professionals in the city are immigrants who, having put enough distance between themselves and the suffocating social structures that kept them in the closet at home, are happy to explore and experiment. When you can meet others of your tribe at the annual Bengaluru Pride or a Queer Campus flea market or around the water cooler at work, a Peacock Drive becomes superfluous.

Much Ado About Nothing comes to the Park, via the Bardolators. The actor in the centre is Danish Sheikh, who also directed and adapted the play.

As for the bamboo groves, those gracious hosts to all the steamy gay action of the decades before the noughties, they have themselves been gone a few years now. But not before they staged one last hurrah as the backdrop to queer adaptations of *Much Ado About Nothing* (2015) and *A Midsummer's Night Dream* (2016). On both occasions, the Bardolators, a theatre group put together by Arvind's colleague in ALF, Danish Sheikh, drew an audience of over 500 to a production of 'Shakespeare in the (Cubbon) Park'. There were no mics, no lights (this was a daytime production), and no sets except for what the park itself provided. As cast member Subhalakshmi Roy put it feelingly in a 2016 blog entry for Rain Tree Media, '…the green field would be our stage, thorny bamboo thickets our green room, and sudden interludes of birdsong our orchestra. Within the sylvan confines of the grove, it is easy to forget the crass cacophony of the city bellowing outside the gates.'

A mesmerised audience that still remembers the day, and the play, as a magical experience, would agree.

*

PS: A bit of historic trivia that may hold the key to the LGBTQIA+ community's affinity for the Park was uncovered by Radha Thomas, jazz singer and author, while she was researching *The Bangalore Monthly*'s September 1998 cover story 'Gay in the Garden City'. A fresco on a pillar flanking the steps leading to the Kacheri's original entrance features two men involved in an intimate sexual encounter!

IN WHICH THE PARK BRINGS A CITY OUT TO RUN AND BIRTHS A TREEHUGGER

> *One Sunday, I was at Bangalore's Cubbon Park when I saw a group of people training for a 10K run, and decided to join them. A year later, I participated in a 10K run. Now running has become an addiction. I am very comfortable running in my hijab. You shouldn't stop yourself just because you are wearing a hijab or a burkha.*
>
> —Asima Sultana, 58, 2020 mascot of the Pinkathon Superwomen's 10K, in finishermag.com

> *Once you hit the main road, runners will take a left for Cubbon Park. You will be running your first 3 km towards the State Library and then take a left from the Dog Park, exiting Cubbon Park at the Century Club exit towards Vidhana Soudha… (The Park) is home to more than 6000 trees. First time runners, take deep breaths in there :))*
>
> —The route of the 2019 Bengaluru Marathon, as described on the website geeksonfeet.com

ARVIND KRISHNAN MOVED TO BANGALORE IN 1999, PART of the early wave of tech immigrants into the city in the wake of the dotcom revolution. 'Two years and I'm out of here,' he remembers thinking to himself as he moved into his rental apartment on Old Airport Road.

Then Bangalore happened to the IIM-C grad. Two years later, he quit his job and turned entrepreneur, founding

The Fuller Life (TFL), an 'employee wellbeing company' that helped other companies create better and more holistic workplaces for their people. Twenty years later, it is India's most experienced company in that space.

Founding TFL helped Arvind rediscover an old love—running. 'The tagline of TFL was "One Life. Do More",' he says. 'It made sense for me to follow that motto myself. At IIM-C, I had run long-distance for joy. I wanted to find that joy again.' He checked with locals about the best places to run in the city, and the answer was always the same. 'Cubbon Park has a way of doing that,' laughs Arvind, 'it forces itself into your orbit, especially if you are not a local.'

So off Arvind went to the Park, with a small group of like-minded friends, to map out a running route. 'We didn't even have to break a sweat—the route presented itself to us, right at the entrance,' laughs Arvind, 'For a long while after that, Cubbon Park to me was the Queen's Park, just that strip between Queen Victoria and Edward VII. There was a track, and we did loops there.'

A Google Group, The Cubbon Park Irregulars, was soon created, and between five and ten people got together each weekend to run. Until, in 2004, long-distance running, and running in general, sprinted its way into India's consciousness with the first-ever organized marathon—Procam's Standard Chartered Mumbai Marathon. The very next year, 2005, TFL had a new offshoot—Runners For Life (RFL). Coincidentally, the inaugural Bengaluru

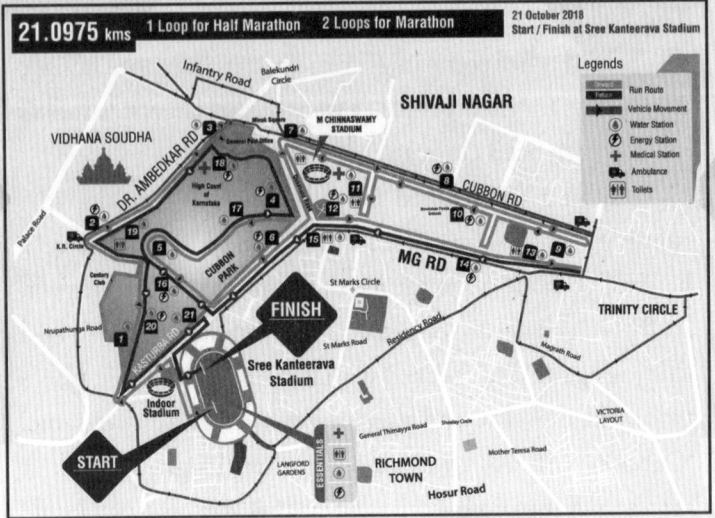

The route map of the 2018 Bengaluru Marathon, with the Half Marathon route itself going through Cubbon Park (the entire shaded area in the centre) twice.

Marathon, which attracted about 200 participants, was held the same year.

As membership to the CP Irregulars swelled slowly but steadily, RFL's monthly organized runs became fortnightly ones, and events like the city's first 10k run—and two of RFL's signature races—Bangalore Ultra, in which participants ran continuously for twenty-four hours, and the iconic Kaveri Trail Marathon, a 42-km course along the banks of the Kaveri in Srirangapatna—were introduced. The success of these encouraged RFL to begin a more serious tryst with running—they moved their sights beyond Bangalore, and were contracted to manage the Nike Run Club for the global fitness major (for eight years, these runs happened in Cubbon Park). They also introduced a third signature running event for corporates, the very successful Urban Stampede. In less than three years after they had first begun operations as a Google Group, RFL had been acknowledged as the pioneers of the running movement in India.

'It was a happy happenstance. We arrived at the right time, both in the city's evolution and running's evolution,' says Arvind. 'And Cubbon Park was just the most obvious place to organize runs.'

Santhosh Padmanabhan, who founded Runners High (RH), a social enterprise that works with disadvantaged children to help them build confidence, self-esteem

Cheered on by traditional drummers, participants in the Bengaluru Marathon begin strongly, passing the State Central Library in Cubbon Park on the first 3-km stretch of the route.

and academic skills through running, agrees. 'From the very beginning, Cubbon Park was the stage. It was 2008, and I had just moved here from the US and started Runners High. My workplace was close to the Park, so I would run there in the mornings and shower at the office before I began work. When we decided to start training runners for a fee, to sustain our social effort, of course we did it in the Park.'

Starting with just ten sign-ups, Runners High now trains over 300 runners in Bangalore alone. Before the pandemic broke, the large and happy group was a common weekend morning sight in the empty parking lot of the High Court, getting their endorphins on before heading out to enjoy the rest of their Sunday. For the last six years, RH has also partnered with neighbourhood residents' welfare associations to provide training support for both beginner and advanced runners.

RFL is no longer involved in organizing running events, but Arvind cannot keep away from the Park. 'You can't avoid it,' he says. 'A long cycle ride or run over the weekend has to involve the Park, because it has to end with breakfast at Airlines or Koshy's or India Coffee House or Konark Kanteerava—that's just tradition.' In 2019, Arvind's then eight-year-old son began to train at the Kanteerava Stadium, right beside the Park. Accompanying parents were politely asked to make themselves scarce for the 90-minute duration. 'My wife and I didn't even pause to think,' he chuckles. 'Who needs a plan when you have Cubbon Park?'

Keen to run again in the Park but loath to stick to the signposted 5-km running route, Arvind charted out a new route for himself—one that made a longer circuit of the Park, hitting all its inclines and declines, and touching each of its eight gates. 'Every gate is a window into the city,' he marvels. 'The kinds of people who walk in through each of them encompass every kind of city resident—the ones who enter from the UB City gate are a whole world apart from those that enter through the Hudson Circle gate, who are again an entirely different breed from those who come in via the Bal Bhavan gate. That's not all, every hour of the day, the demographics change. As an immigrant, I have discovered Bangalore through the locus of the Park.'

Time was when there weren't as many people coming through. Asha Mokashi, who moved to the city in 1992 to teach French at the Department of Foreign Languages at Bangalore University, remembers the tree cover being far less dense than it is now. She didn't visit the Park much; back then, it didn't feel safe for a lone woman. Even in the daytime, she remembers being accosted by 'shady characters' asking if she wanted drugs. It was only around 2010 that she started visiting regularly with her friends.

'I think it was the runners who changed the atmosphere,' she says. 'They were mostly young immigrants who were into fitness and needed somewhere to convene over the weekends because they didn't have family here. When they discovered the Park, they began to bring their spouses and children along.'

The runners certainly helped, but there were also other forces at play. After Bangalore came together as one in 1998 to protest the denotification of 32 acres of the Park, activist judges like Justice Michael Saldanha and citizen petitioners like theatre person Bimal Desai and Umesh Kumar ensured that fences came up around the Park's perimeter, rallies and film shootings were banned inside, and Park gates were shut to traffic between 10 p.m. and 8 a.m. There was more. The year 2004 heralded the emergence of a mega-influencer, the likes of which the world had never seen before. 'Facebook!' exclaims Asha. 'It only needed one person to post a picture of *Tabebuia impetiginosa* in bloom in Ringwood Circle for young people to begin arriving in droves.' More recently, street lights, security cameras, and regular policing have made the Park even safer.

'Oh, absolutely,' agrees Santhosh. 'Even as late as 2008, I used to be cat-called and heckled when I came through on my long runs at 4 a.m. Now, even a lone woman running in the Park at 5 a.m. is unlikely to be bothered by anyone.'

By 2006, Asha, who had by now moved from teaching French to technical writing, had fallen so deeply in love with Cubbon Park that when she had to choose between two job offers, she chose the one that would allow her to drive through the Park each day. She followed that up with a resolution to never live further than fifteen minutes' driving distance from the Park, even if that meant, inevitably, a much higher rent. Turning evangelist, she brought friends and colleagues to the Park, organizing picnics and volunteer meets, and participating in painting sessions under the trees. And if her visiting foreign bosses ever let slip that they thought Bangalore was a concrete jungle ('To be fair,' chuckles Asha, 'I would have said the same if I had been put up in a hotel on the Outer Ring Road'), she dragged them from one end of the Park to another until they acknowledged its magnificence and begged for mercy.

Asha didn't know it then, but Cubbon Park would return her love in equal measure. In 2015, she received a devastating diagnosis of pre-glaucoma, and had to go through painful eye surgeries that took months to heal. For an entire year, terrified that she would lose her vision, Asha came to visit a particular silk cotton tree at the Park. 'I used to hug it and tell it all my fears and pray to it,' she says. 'It was truly where my gods resided.' Again, within a span of four months in 2018, she was hit with a series of health setbacks—her father was diagnosed with cancer, and her husband suffered two heart attacks. Her world was falling apart, but the silk cotton stood, steadfast.

'Watching the tree come back to life after shedding all its leaves was a great lesson in hope and renewal,' she says. 'The tree and the Park, they resurrected me.' Grateful beyond measure for the grace she had received, Asha paid tribute to the Park through a series of beautiful, moving pieces of writing on her blog, whiletheworldisgoingplaces.blogspot.com.

'Everyone thinks of Cubbon Park as Bangalore's centre,' she smiles. 'I'd put it a little differently—Cubbon Park centres Bangalore.'

The Guardians

IN WHICH THE PARK WELCOMES THE CITY TO SENSATIONAL SUNDAYS

The music concerts at Cubbon Park triggered controversy about eight years ago when a section of joggers raised objections that it would disturb the morning serenity and peaceful ambience. However, following repeated requests by walkers and consultation with experts that such music concerts would not disturb others and the surrounding environment, the government has reintroduced the morning musical concerts. Sources in the government clarified that only classical and light classical music would be allowed during the concert.

—Niranjan Kaggere, reporting for *Bangalore Mirror*, 31 May 2015

A five-month-old baby has approached the High Court seeking a ban on vehicular traffic within and through Cubbon Park. Kian Medhi Kumar, represented by his father M.R. Rakesh Prabal Kumar, cited drastic reduction in air pollution during the lockdown to seek a permanent ban on traffic in the city's premier lung space. Between March 24 and May 20, when the lockdown was in force, there was a reduction of suspended particulate matter and carbon monoxide level inside Cubbon Park, he stated.

—Report in *Deccan Herald*, 25 December 2020

IN AUGUST 2013, EXACTLY TWO WEEKS AFTER MAHANTESH Murgod took over as deputy director in Karnataka's Horticulture Department with the charge of Cubbon Park, the Karnataka Legislative Council adopted the Karnataka Government Parks (Preservation) (Amendment) Bill, removing 49 acres and 34 guntas of land from within the ambit of the Park. Just two months previously, a new Indian National Congress-led government under Mr Siddaramaiah had been sworn in, following five years of a mired-in-controversy BJP regime during which three different Chief Ministers had held sway. Eager to reclaim Vidhana Soudha by installing statues of Congress leaders like Lal Bahadur Shastri and Mahatma Gandhi on the grounds, the new government came up against an old, old problem—because Vidhana Soudha and several other government buildings around it were deemed to be part of Cubbon Park, no new constructions or installations were permitted there, according to the provisions of the Parks (Preservation) Act of 1975. The Amendment Bill had been hanging fire for years; on 31 July 2013, it was passed within minutes by a voice vote, with the full support of the Opposition.

Instead of losing sleep over the loss of such a large area

under his jurisdiction, Mahantesh decided to focus his energies on making the 197 acres that were still within the boundaries of Cubbon Park as wonderful—and seductive—an urban green resource as possible. 'It is only when the people of a city use it that any public space truly becomes part of the city's consciousness,' he says. 'Everyone knew of the Park, but mostly as a thoroughfare that they drove through. I wanted people, both new immigrants and old Bangaloreans, to come in with their families, spend time here, enjoy it. Only if people have good memories of a space will they do their bit to protect and preserve it.'

With the backing of his boss, Joint Director (Parks & Gardens) Dr M Jagadeesh, Mahantesh went to work. 'A large area of the Park, especially the area between the Hudson Circle Gate and the Siddalingaiah Circle gate, was in bad shape—overgrown, unused, inaccessible to walkers,' remembers Jagadeesh, who had briefly served as deputy director, Cubbon Park, before Mahantesh took over, and had been instrumental in commissioning the restoration of heritage structures like the bandstand and the fairy fountain. 'It had become a scary place to walk past after dark, sheltering all kinds of criminal elements. We started with clearing up the undergrowth and trimming tree branches that were too close to the ground, thus opening up the area visually. Then we set about laying a paved walkers' path there, with proper kerbs and everything. By the time we were done, there was 5.5 km of paved walking track that wound through the entire park and ensured a smooth walk, even for senior citizens.'

That brought the walkers trickling in, but Mahantesh knew he needed something more dramatic to make citizens sit up and take notice. It was true that with the city expanding beyond anyone's imagination, both in size and population, since the late '90s, and the inevitable traffic congestion it had brought in its wake, the problem of access to the Park was a real thing. But with two Metro stations—Cubbon Park and Dr BR Ambedkar—slated to open on the Park's periphery, that problem would soon be

Since 2015, when the Sunday traffic ban came into force as the result of a citizen intervention, the Park has become even more popular with runners, walkers and cyclists.

a thing of the past. He had a small window of opportunity before that happened to create a buzz. That was when KR Harinarayan, who had moved to the city in the late '90s and lived close to the Park, walked into his office with a proposal after his own heart.

'The refreshing thing about Mahantesh,' says Harinarayan, 'was that he kept himself accessible to citizens. I told him about how some of the Cubbon Park entrances, like the one near Bal Bhavan, which had been closed to traffic for years until the Metro work began, had remained open even after most of the heavy work had been completed. I explained that as someone who regularly ran in the Park, I actually felt the difference that open gate made to the levels of pollution inside. My proposal to him was that the Park be closed to traffic permanently, and if that wasn't possible, at least on the weekends.'

The idea of a traffic-free Cubbon Park was not a new one. It had been petitioned for many times, and by many people over the years (and continues to be, as the excerpt from a 2020 news report at the beginning of this chapter shows). It was also one of Mahantesh's own pet projects, and the timing was perfect. Promising to do his best, he requested Hari to garner citizen and press support, and set about tackling the rest of his department, the administration, and the biggest stumbling block to all such proposals in the past—the Bangalore traffic police.

'The police have always been against the idea of banning

traffic through the Park,' says civic activist Priya Chetty-Rajagopal, who has, among other things, consistently campaigned for the preservation of Bangalore's heritage, green and otherwise. 'They claim it would cause too much congestion in the streets around, and that lawyers, judges and politicians need to use these roads to get to their places of work quickly. But we've done a distance comparison using routes through the Park, versus around the Park, to get to the High Court and the Vidhana Soudha, and the difference between the two routes is never more than 0.6 km.'

That kind of logic had never impressed the police, and it didn't this time around either. But Mahantesh's determined chipping away at their resistance, and the over 1000 real (as opposed to virtual) signatures that Hari had managed to collect from citizens, ensured that they unbent far enough to agree to permanently shut those gates through which there was low traffic flow. They also—hallelujah!—agreed to close the Park entirely to traffic on Sundays, strictly on a trial basis. If the response from the city was tepid, the police were quick to add, they would pull the scheme.

Jubilant, Mahantesh put together all the bells and whistles he considered essential to a great family outing—bicycles on hire, music and dance performances in the bandstand, kiosks selling millets and organic vegetables, a plant nursery, a coffee-tea-toast stall set up by the Coffee Board ('We didn't want to offer any more food than that because of the potential litter') and crossed his fingers, hoping Bangalore would come.

And Bangalore did. Through the Sunday of 24 May 2015, and every Sunday that followed until the pandemic hit, students, couples and families poured in to reclaim their city's verdant heart. Nostalgia served as a great incentive—thousands of adults who visited came because of happy, sepia-tinted memories of childhood Sunday afternoons spent in the adjacent Bal Bhavan grounds. The glowing reports in the press, and word of mouth via social media, did the rest. To Mahantesh's ears, the sweetest sound was the happy shrieking of children learning to ride a bicycle for the first time, helped by parents who felt comfortable letting them go, knowing that they were in no danger from vehicular traffic.

The Principal Secretary, Horticulture, Rajeev Chawla, who himself was present to take in the atmosphere that first Sunday, was so impressed that he personally liaised with every concerned department and the chief minister to ensure that the temporary order for traffic-free Park Sundays was converted into a permanent one. Three months later, Mahantesh, Hari, and the citizens of Bangalore also won their bid for traffic-free second Saturdays (when both government offices and software companies are shut for business) at the Park, and even later, traffic-free national holidays. For the deputy director, it was both a professional triumph and a personal one.

But Mahantesh was far from done. During his six-year tenure, roads and fences and street lights throughout the Park were repaired, toilet blocks constructed, the statue of Queen Victoria restored (in partnership with the state archaeological department), signage detailing the Park's history, trees, birds, and extent, put up, and fallen trees, which the Forest Department used to take ages to move out of the Park, converted into sculptures ('We organized a fifteen-day workshop for artists with the Karnataka Shilpakala Academy, and you can see the work they produced—between thirty and forty pieces—all over the Park today').

A Bharatanatyam performance in progress at the bandstand, part of the traffic-free Sundays' morning experience.

There was one more thing. It troubled Mahantesh no end that the name of the Park did not feature at any of its entrance gates. To remedy that, he had a former PWD architect design two grand arches—one at the High Court entrance to the Park, with a design matching the Attara Kacheri's neoclassical design, and another at the Hudson Circle entrance, to match the architectural style of the State Central Library. Both carried on them, in the best inclusive traditions of the Park, both its names: its official 'City' name, Sri Chamarajendra Park, and its given 'Cantonment' name, Cubbon Park.

The Warriors

IN WHICH TWO DOUGHTY PARK CRUSADERS BRING A CITY TO ITS FEET

The pond near the High Court has been the site of dumping of the rubble from its extension. The 80 ft moat around the Venkatappa Art Gallery has served as convenient repository for debris for the construction activity at the Kanteerava Stadium and the bamboo groves nearby have been gouged out of the fertile soil with no more respect than weeds from a vegetable patch.

And that's not all of it: everywhere around the once-virginal Cubbon Park, there is flotsam and jetsam, human waste from political rallies, heaps of non-biodegradable refuse, useless lamp posts, broken fencing and the stumps of trees that stand as truncated testimonials to the delinquency of the Park authorities.

The experts say that at the present rate of degradation, they do not give the park more than 15 years of survival, unless Justice Saldanha's orders are implemented immediately.

—Ramjee Chandran, editor and publisher, Explocity.com, in 'The Conspiracy to Kill Cubbon Park', *The Bangalore Monthly*, May 1996

When Justice Michael F Saldanha of the venerable Bombay High Court arrived in Bangalore in July 1994 to take over his new role as Justice of the Karnataka High Court, it was something of a homecoming. Born and brought up in Mangalore, the gold medallist in English from Mysore University had moved to Bombay at the age of twenty, to pursue a degree in law. Now, with close to thirty years of legal experience under his belt, and only ten years away from retirement, he was determined to make an impact in his home state. As he walked into his new chambers inside the Attara Kacheri, the 126-year-old heritage building that abutted the Cubbon Park, he had no idea how soon that opportunity would come.

A few months after Justice Saldanha had taken charge, well-known Bangalore theatre actor and entrepreneur Bimal Desai found himself in a particularly dark mood as he headed home to Race Course Road, after his usual morning run in Cubbon Park. Four years previously, the government had taken up the construction of an annexe to the Attara Kacheri. Considering that the heritage structure had escaped demolition just ten years earlier*, this new construction was a good thing. It meant that the Kacheri was safe from

---

*In March 1982, the government of Karnataka, claiming that the 116-year-old Attara Kacheri's structural stability was precarious, approved its demolition. What the government had not anticipated, in its wildest dreams, was a spirited resistance from the Bangalore citizenry. In a never-before move, a group of prominent Bangaloreans led by filmmaker

the wrecking ball for years to come. Bimal understood and appreciated that; what drove him around the bend were the tonnes of debris being dumped into the Park.

Over the years, under his very nose, dozens of Park trees had been sacrificed to clear space for the annexe, and the pond inside the Court premises had vanished under the construction debris, never to return. That morning, when he locked eyes with a broken, stained commode sitting on a mound of rubble, something snapped. Turning to his running partner, MG Kumar, who was also an advocate, Bimal asked if he could help him file a PIL in the High Court, seeking the removal of debris, and demanding the maintenance and preservation of the Park.

By the time the actor-turned-crusader's PIL was filed in June 1995, Justice Saldanha, who also enjoyed taking his morning and post-lunch constitutional in the Park, had begun to feel his own blood pressure rising at its state. His

---

M Bhaktavatsala, architect PK Venkataramanan of Venkataramanan Associates, and the then chairperson of INTACH, Naomi Meadows, filed the state's very first Public Interest Litigation (PIL) against the proposed move. That PIL, which was heard in the very building due for demolition, pleaded that the Attara Kacheri was 'a precious cultural heritage… (whose) destruction snaps an emotional experience vital to a sense of belonging to this beautiful city.' The High Court struck down the petition, but expressed sympathy with the petitioners. Encouraged, the petitioners appealed against the decision in the Supreme Court, which asked the state government to reconsider its proposal. In 1985, bowing to the Court's recommendation and public opinion, the government dropped the idea, investing instead in the heritage building's restoration.

Ramjee Chandran

The May 1996 issue of *The Bangalore Monthly* featured a young theatre artist-turned-activist called Bimal Desai. His fight to save Cubbon Park, which began in 1994, would go on for years, and include as many victories as losses.

ire was not so much about the debris but about Cubbon Park being the city's preferred venue for political rallies, given that it was right opposite the Vidhana Soudha. 'Thousands of people from outside the city would be bussed in for these rallies, and let loose in the Park,' remembers the Justice. 'They would hack away at tree branches for firewood to cook their meals, and use the Park as an open toilet.'

That wasn't all. 'There were also film shootings happening constantly, with their large crews, and even larger crowd of rubberneckers. The timber mafia, in collusion with the Horticulture Department, were helping themselves merrily, under cover of darkness, to all the sandalwood and teak in the Park. And if you greased the right palms, you would be allowed to graze your cattle in the Park at night. It was a terrible situation.' Meanwhile, realizing that his PIL would take its own sweet time through the legal process, Bimal went to see Justice Saldanha to plead his cause. It was an instant meeting of minds. In March 1996, on Bimal's urging, the Justice wrote a strongly worded letter to the state governor, Khurshed Alam Khan, accusing the Horticulture Department, the PWD, and the Cubbon Park police of not taking cognisance of the damage to the Park over the years, and asking Khan to take immediate action against the felling of trees and dumping of debris. The letter was widely circulated in the press.

Reassured that the battle had been escalated to the highest level, Bimal continued doing what he was best at. 'I simply filed more PILs, hoping something would click,' he says. 'When a cyclist was fatally hit by a scooter, I filed one to ban traffic in the Park; when construction of the Kanteerava Indoor Stadium, which was being readied for the 1997 National Games, resulted in the dumping of more construction debris in the moat around the Venkatappa Art Gallery on Kasturba Road, I filed a PIL against that; frustrated by the litter around every hawker's cart, I filed a PIL to disallow vending inside the Park; when I noticed that the Bal Bhavan lake was silting up, I filed one against the blocking of the Park's natural water channels—you have to be creative with this stuff.'

Alongside, Bimal tried other tacks, like meeting with the officials at the Venkatappa Art Gallery to request them to preserve the moat. 'It wasn't about the moat so much as preserving the Park's natural drainage channels around which Richard Sankey had designed these water bodies,' he explains. 'By blocking the channels, we were not only ruining the Park's aesthetics, we were permanently destroying its water table.'

The gallery officials had no time for him, however. Bimal then approached the Thoreau Foundation, a centre for environmental, intellectual and humanitarian activities, whose experts instantly saw both the merits in, and the urgency of, Bimal's argument. They petitioned Justice Saldanha separately, urging him to use every power available to him to take quick action.

Convinced, the good judge went to work. In April 1996, he issued a series of suo moto orders, banning political rallies and tree felling in the Park, ordering the replenishment of all four ponds by clearing them of silt within forty-five days, and demanding an explanation from the state government and the police for the sad state of law and order within the Park. Taken by surprise, the government blustered for a bit but eventually caved, permanently banning political rallies in the Park.

That was just the beginning. Next to be packed off were hawkers and film crews. A fence came up around the Park, and gates were shut to traffic each day between 10 p.m. and

8 a.m. Given that the Park was too large to be patrolled effectively by police on foot, policemen on bicycles were brought in. On the Justice's orders, a fenced-in area within the Park was set aside for the police to impound any stray cattle grazing in the park. 'That fenced-in area,' chuckles the octogenarian, 'is today Cubbon Park's famous Dog Park!'

Bimal was delighted, but he knew the fight was far from over. In 1997, the Legislator's Home (LH), just outside the Park fences, began building an annexe, in wilful violation of the law—the LH lay within the boundaries of the Park, where no new construction was permitted. Once again, Bimal filed a PIL, and a long and grim battle ensued. It ended, temporarily, with Justice Saldanha issuing a stay order on the construction.

In that charged atmosphere, even government departments caught the activist bug. The Forest Department turned down a proposal by the Century Club* to cut down two prized trees to build a new office block. When the KSLTA (Karnataka State Lawn Tennis Association) proposed a Rs 16-lakh construction project in their tennis

---

*A private gentleman's club, founded in 1917, with exactly one hundred members (which explains its name) by the erstwhile dewan of Mysore, Sir M Visvesvaraya. So cut up was Sir MV when he was refused entry into the Cantonment's Bangalore Club wearing his trademark Mysore peta (turban) that he determined to create a space where distinguished Indians, wearing Indian clothes, could meet and exchange ideas. The maharaja was entirely on his side. The Century Club came up on seven acres of land inside Cubbon Park, generously granted by the maharaja.

court within the Park, to enable the live telecast of the tennis matches during the 1997 National Games, the Directorate of Horticulture requested the chief minister to disallow it. When the government proposed turning part of the Park into a parking lot during the Games, the police not only did not give permission, but refused to allow parking along any of the roads inside the Park as well.

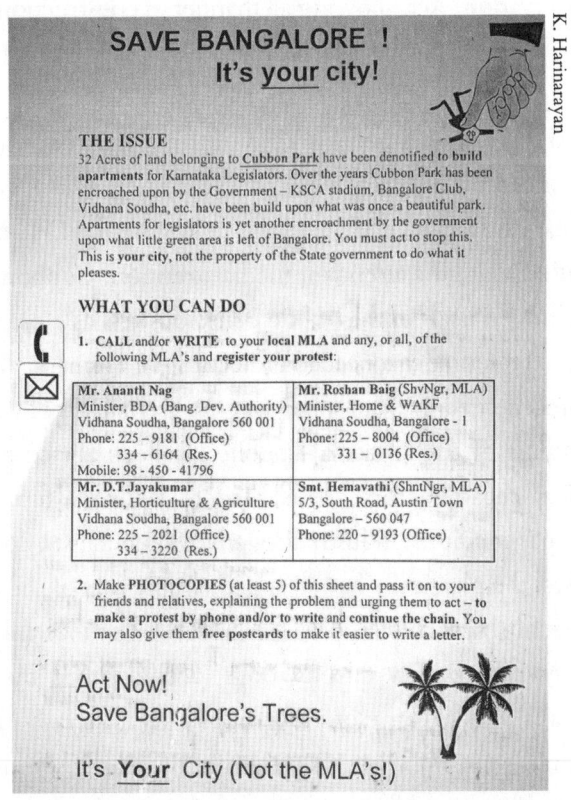

A public awareness leaflet from the 1998 protests, urging people to participate in reclaiming Cubbon Park.

In 1998, frustrated at every turn by the indefatigable citizen petitioner and the ornery judge, and determined to complete the LH annexe, the state government decided to denotify 32 acres of the Park. Those 32 (or 44, depending on who you asked) acres contained in them most of the government buildings around the Park. The denotification would free those areas forever from the strictures of the Parks (Preservation) Act, allowing all manner of construction very close to the Park's periphery. Needless to say, Bimal filed a PIL against the move.

At any other time, this kind of thing may have passed unnoticed by ordinary citizens. Over the previous couple of years, however, and especially following the LH annexe brouhaha and the attendant media attention, Cubbon Park had lodged itself in the public consciousness as a precious, beloved resource that needed protecting. In a remarkable and unprecedented show of solidarity, representatives of various segments of the citizenry—public intellectuals, corporate leaders, theatre actors, artists, writers, Kannada film stars, newspaper editors, industrialists, environmentalists, doctors, nurses, the physically handicapped, employees of the city's blue-chip software companies, NGOs, schoolchildren, housewives, beauty queens, dogs (accompanied by their humans), and even esoteric groups like the Hash House Harriers—most of them drawn from the usually somnolent and apathetic middle class, assembled, in a relay fashion, at the statue of Queen Vic, day after day, for six full weeks over September and October, to be part of the 'Save Cubbon Park' campaign. In parallel, a group of experts volunteered to conduct a census of the Park's biodiversity, to raise public awareness of what would be lost if the denotification went through.

'I still get goosebumps when I think about it,' smiles Bimal. 'The first indication I had that this fight was going to be different was when I received a call from a lady who had read about me in the papers, and was wondering if I would go over and address her kitty party group and give them details about the issue at hand. I did so, and members of the group came and sat at the statue every single day after that. The second indication was when the famous Kannada actress, Bharathi Vishnuvardhan, turned up at the protest site one day, unannounced.'

But it was the press that was the fight's biggest ally. TJS George, then editor of the *Indian Express*, ensured that the protest was on the paper's front page every day for a month. Bimal himself was hardly ever at the protest site—he was all over town giving talks at schools, colleges, corporates, clubs, recruiting fresh blood to the cause. 'You must remember this was a time before social media,' says Bimal, 'and yet our signature campaigns garnered over one lakh signatures from ordinary citizens.'

Expectedly, the authorities eventually found a way to shut the protests down. 'Saldanha was shifted off the case,' remembers Bimal, 'and the PIL was taken up for deliberation by the court. Once the case is sub judice, protests become illegal. At some point, a judgement in favour of the denotification was passed.'

Bimal lost that case, but the support he had received from his city so energized him that he continued to fight for Cubbon Park via the legal route for many years longer, filing fourteen PILs in all, many of which he lost. A little sadder, but a lot wiser, he now contributes to his city not so much by trying to protect the green cover it still has, but by adding to it. He does this by creating urban forests across Bangalore for whoever wants it, using the Miyawaki method. 'It's never too late to stop complaining and start doing,' he smiles. 'We can reverse the damage that has been done to our city—all it requires is will power.'

As for Justice Saldanha, he had many more laurels awaiting him before he retired in 2004. Apart from being rated one of the world's Top Ten judges by the International Jurists' Association, it was his judgements on alternative fuels between 1998 and 1999 that were instrumental in getting the Supreme Court to issue directions for conversion of all public transport to CNG. Unapologetic and outspoken as ever, the octogenarian is still called upon to lend his voice to citizens' protests, and gladly does. 'If I can make Bangalore a better place to live in,' he says simply, 'I will.'

IN WHICH THE PARK GOES TO THE DOGS

> *Even those humans who are evidently not fond of dogs behave themselves in the precincts of the park. They had better. For, at least in the morning hours, animal-lovers are in a majority here. In the hours when it is closed to vehicular traffic (before 8 a.m.), when the elite of Central Bangalore take a stroll, Cubbon Park is an undeclared sanctuary for animals, especially dogs, both pet and stray.*
>
> —N Bhanutej, writing in the *Economic Times*,
> 28 September 2018

> *Held a meeting with Horticulture Minister Shri @ MunirathnaMLA concerning a proposal to prohibit the entry of pet dogs into #Bengaluru's #Cubbon Park (from July 1, 2022). The Horticulture department temporarily blocks the ban on pets. Hon Minister assured me that he would look into this matter.*
>
> —PC Mohan, third time MP from Bangalore Central Constituency, on Twitter, 28 June 2022

FOR MOST OF HER LIFE, PRIYA CHETTY-RAJAGOPAL WAS terrified of dogs. It wasn't until she lost her dog-loving mother in the late 1990s that, completely distraught, she even considered bringing a pup home. She mentioned the thought casually to a few friends, never dreaming that they would take her seriously. One fine day very soon after, she found that she had become mum to an energetic black-and-white bundle of spaniel that she had no idea how to handle. Priya needn't have worried—CJ, aka Calamity Jane, knew exactly how to handle her. A few weeks in, human and dog were deeply and inextricably in love.

For CJ's sake, Priya returned to a childhood haunt, Cubbon Park. Together, the two explored the green vistas each weekend, and made a lot of doggie friends, mainly the strays that lived in the Park. When CJ passed in 2013, the same overwhelming feeling of loss and grief that had assailed Priya at her mum's death returned. 'There was no reason to go back to Cubbon Park,' she says, 'but I couldn't keep away—maybe I thought that talking to her friends there would keep her memory alive, maybe I felt closest to her when I was back in the Park... I'm not sure what it was. It certainly made me think about the strays, though, and it made me want to do something concrete for "CJ's friends".'

Bangalore's favourite cartoonist Nala Ponnappa has weighed in more than once on happenings in Cubbon Park. This particular cartoon was the inspiration for the 'Knights of Cubbon Bark', a group of concerned citizens who would represent the Park dogs and their rights.

That's when Priya began to connect to other humans who cared about the strays—people like Kumkum Malhotra, Jyoti Thyagarajan, and Sunita Kumar, who had been feeding the Cubbon Park strays for years. It was their dedicated efforts that had ensured the Park strays were calmer and friendlier than most—secure in the knowledge that they would not go hungry, they did not bother visitors, human or canine, or fight amongst themselves. It struck Priya that while there was an enormous amount of heart in Bangalore where animal welfare was concerned, it was more a collection of scattered individual contributions than an organized, holistic effort at a community level.

'Although the strays were well-fed, they were always in danger,' she explains. 'From disease, from traffic, from people who didn't like dogs. They had no one to fight for their rights. On the flip side, the walkers had no protection from the dogs, either, which made them (the walkers) hostile. What was needed was a platform where people from both sides could gather, and advocacy could be done. I decided to create that platform, with Cubbon Park as its storefront.'

Thus was born, in 2014, the CJ Memorial Trust, along with the Facebook group The Cubbon Park Canines (CPC). 'Branding and visibility are important,' explains Priya. 'We decided the dogs in the Park would no longer be just "Park dogs" or "Park strays", they would be "Parkies". Drawing inspiration from a Ponnappa cartoon, the core group of humans who would represent them and their rights were named the "Knights of Cubbon Bark".'

Since their initiation, the Knights have had their work cut out for them. In 2015, the Horticulture Department toyed with the idea of banning pet dogs from the Park—two weeks later, a petition against the move supported by over 2000 citizen signatures was submitted to the department, forcing them to abandon it. Later the same year, when citizen petitions finally succeeded in making the Park traffic-free on Sundays, the Knights lobbied hard and got the department to assign a largish fenced-in area next to the Public Library for pet dogs, where they could run off-leash. Now, each Sunday, there are almost as many people along the fence looking into the Dog Park—timid children who want to enjoy the large variety of dogs from a safe distance, families contemplating bringing a puppy home and looking for tips, out-of-towners who come seeking this unique tourist hotspot—as there are inside. 'Actress Asha Parekh visited a few years ago,' smiles Priya. 'She said she had heard about this "paradise on earth" in Bangalore and could not leave without dropping in.'

Priya has lost count of the number of city-wide campaigns the Knights have launched in the last eight years from the soapbox of the Dog Park and the CPC Facebook page (now at 16.3k members). Since the page's initiation, the #BanOnlinePetSales national initiative has taken about 3000 illegally bred pups offline, i.e., forced ecommerce websites to stop the sale of pups. The group's openly articulated anti-breeder stance—'In here, it is indies (native dog breeds and mongrels) and rescues (dogs that have been rescued from labs, neglectful owners or abandonment, and later adopted) that get the red carpet rolled out for them—has naturally put some people off. But it has slowly but very surely created a culture of adoption over purchase and indies over foreign breeds among the city's dog lovers. The 'DogTagged, Not DogGone' campaign has distributed over 16,000 dog tags for free, to ensure there are fewer lost dogs.

Working with the Bangalore municipality, the BBMP, the Dog Park has hosted pet licensing camps, so that pet dogs are registered with the city corporation. 'We are very happy to cooperate with the city municipality and use our platform to not only amplify their rules but ensure compliance in the Park where dogs are concerned,' says Priya. 'That is why there is such a sense of anger and betrayal when they blindside us with some ridiculous new rule.' One such episode occurred in 2018, when the BBMP proposed a bylaw that limited the number of pet dogs per apartment to one, and per independent house to three. The kind of furore that erupted among animal activists and dog lovers across the city, backing Priya's NotWithoutMyDog hashtag, was strident enough for the civic body to withdraw its plans almost immediately.

As for the Parkies, the CPC page, by telling their

The CJ Memorial Trust Facebook page

A common Sunday scene in the Dog Park. With both the Horticulture Department and members of the public not entirely convinced about letting pet dogs into the Park, how much longer such scenes will play out is anyone's guess.

stories and posting their pictures, has ensured that they are celebrities in their own right. In the early days, the Knights even organized 'Parkie spotting' walks for interested visitors. But it isn't all cuddle-and-fuzz. 'Everyone comes to the Santa Bow Wow, our annual Christmas party in the Dog Park, sees me in my Yuletide bonhomie and tinsel, and may see a privileged, English-speaking woman having fun,' says Priya. 'But there is also so much heartbreak, and so much hard work the Knights do.'

Like regularly taking time off work, vet in tow, to 'capture' Parkies and ensure they are all vaccinated. Or haranguing the BBMP to ensure every Parkie is spayed or neutered. 'We haven't had a single birth in the Park for four years now,' confirms Priya. Or negotiating with the police to allow responsible 'feeders' into the Park through the COVID lockdowns, so that the Parkies did not go hungry. Or getting speed-limit signs put up to keep Parkies safe from hit-and-run accidents. Or advocating for strict fines to be imposed on irresponsible pet dog owners for not leashing their dogs or picking up their poop. 'We want dogs to be welcomed in the community, not reviled,' says Priya, 'and that happens only with more civic sense and responsibility from us animal lovers.'

One of Priya's biggest wins, the establishment of the Karnataka Animal Welfare Board (KAWB) in 2019, was the result of years of online campaigns and lobbying with various chief ministers by the CJ Memorial Trust. 'Can you believe we didn't have one? That every state should have an AWB that functions under the Animal Welfare Board of India, and that every district in a state should further have an SPCA (Society for the Prevention of Cruelty to Animals), has been clearly stipulated by the Supreme Court as far back as 2001, but we had neither!'* Eight months after the KAWB was set up, all thirty-one districts of Karnataka had SPCAs as well. 'The SPCA and the KAWB give our campaigns teeth, they give us a structure from where we can take a stance and do what is right.'

---

*Ironical, considering that the Bangalore SPCA was established as far back as 1888, and registered formally over a century ago, in 1916! Today, it goes by the name of the Karuna Animal Welfare Association of Karnataka, but part of it is still housed in the quaint little cottage that was the original BSPCA building, at the Bal Bhavan entrance of Cubbon Park.

As far as Cubbon Park is concerned, the battle, as can be gauged from the second quote at the beginning of this chapter, is never over. But the determined efforts of Priya and her Knights over the last eight years have raised the consciousness of an already dog-loving city to a new and more focused pitch, one that will be difficult to tone down in a hurry. How does it feel to be an inspiration? Priya laughs. 'I often get the feeling that I'm the most hated person in the world. Dog owners hate me because I'm always yelling at them to leash their dogs or pick up after them, walkers hate me because they believe I'm only on the side of the dogs, animal activists hate me because I see the administration's point of view, the administration hates me because I'm always on their case about something, breeders hate me because, well, I hate them. Basically, I can't win.'

In the eyes of more than one generation of Parkies, and hundreds of pet dogs (and their owners), she already has.

IN WHICH A ONE-MAN ARMY RESURRECTS A BELOVED COMMISSIONER

> *I am an environmentalist. To protect this park is my dharma. Cubbon Park-na runa tindiddeevalla, maadbeku! (We owe a great debt to Cubbon Park. We must do what it takes!)*
>
> —S Umesh Kumar, Senior High Court Advocate and President of the Cubbon Park Walkers' Association

> *Umesh and the association represent a particular breed of civic activism that is gaining precedence in the discourse around*

public space. The association members' imagination of the park evokes visions of high fences and manicured enclosures where any experience of this park would be mediated through licenses, permits and registrations. This innocuous sounding blueprint of the gentrification of the park excludes an entire community of people who for decades have accessed it for various purposes.

—Angarika Guha and Shruthi Menon of the media and arts collective Maraa, in their essay 'Cubbon Park Symbolises the Contestation over Bangalore's Public Spaces', published in *The Wire* in December 2016

UMESH KUMAR'S TRYST WITH CUBBON PARK BEGAN IN 1986, the year he was admitted to the University Law College, Bangalore, as a boy of eighteen. The college is part of Bangalore University's City Campus on Post Office Road, less than 500 m from the Park's western boundary.

As a law student, Umesh spent a lot of time in Cubbon Park. Power outages were all too common at the hostel, and the Park provided a cool, green sanctuary for shooting the breeze with classmates, or hunkering down for frantic 'group study' sessions before the exams. It also provided a great backdrop for heated debates about unfair college policies, and thereon to planning protests and rebellion against the authorities. Within a few months of joining the course, Umesh had taken on the mantle of 'student leader', and was spending his days battling with the college establishment on behalf of every aggrieved student, becoming, in his own words, 'the voice of the voiceless'.

'It was really heart-breaking,' he says of his fellow students who came from extremely straitened circumstances. 'The food at the hostel mess was free, but often terrible, and these kids could not afford to eat anywhere else. There was also the bigger problem of language—we all knew a little English, but there was no way they—or I, even—would be able to write an exam in that language. And yet, there was no other option.' In his six years there, while he petitioned the college authorities for better food at the mess, Umesh personally funded wholesome meals for some of the worse-off students. He also led a sustained campaign for the right to choose to write exams in Kannada, and won. It was a landmark victory for his own classmates and for every batch that came after.

If that initial success with challenging authority set him on the path to what he is today—an untiring and secular PIL-filer against any number of violations against the city by the crooked, no matter how rich or famous or powerful they may be—the happy, productive hours spent in Cubbon Park built his deep and abiding love for it. His proximity to the Park, both physical and emotional, did not diminish even after he had graduated, for his new theatre of operations lay just a kilometre down the road, at the Karnataka High Court.

*

Umesh's Park-related activism began in 2012, when he read a news item about an unidentified person who had been found dead there in mysterious circumstances. 'It had not escaped my notice that over the years, the Park had become a haven for all kinds of soliciting—by eunuchs, prostitutes, petty criminals, drug peddlers,' recalls Umesh. 'But that news item was the trigger. I realized it was up to common citizens like me, who cared for irreplaceable public spaces like Cubbon Park, to take up for it.'

Always a believer in the dictum that strength lies in numbers, Umesh quickly drew up a charter for a citizens' group called the Cubbon Park Walkers' Association (CPWA). Of the 2000 fully signed-up members, many were powerful and influential people who lived and worked in the area, and were, as a result, regular walkers in the Park. That done, the CPWA issued identity cards to their members and other walkers, and began petitioning the Horticulture Department for a slew of what they believed were necessary and desirable changes to the Park.

One of the first demands of the CPWA, in 2013, was that the Park be fenced more robustly. The Association even went so far as to offer to raise money from citizens and do it themselves. 'It's ridiculous how much care and concern is extended to Lalbagh by the Horticulture Department,' says Umesh. 'It has a boundary wall, security guards, two grand flower shows each year, ticketed entry...But Cubbon Park, even though it is surrounded by powerful people and institutions, or perhaps because of the self-serving agendas of those institutions, is only seen as a place to take from, not give back to.' By 2015, the Park was re-fenced.

Umesh and the CPWA are also determined not to surrender another inch of what is left of the Park to construction or other illegal activities. Since 1988, five amendments made to the original Parks (Preservation) Act of 1975 have redrawn and shrunk the boundaries of the Park, most recently to accommodate the pillars and stations of the Bangalore Metro. 'In the '80s, the Park sprawled across 300 acres, now it has shrunk to 197,' says an indignant Umesh. 'That's not all. Large parts of those 197 acres are not available to the public, because they are fenced off for use by private and government institutions. It goes without saying that these institutions will violate the strictures of the Act, which prohibits all additions or extensions to existing structures, the instant we take our eyes off them.'

And so, Umesh performs his dharma—protecting the Park—by filing PILs against the offending parties. Currently pending in court are cases against several institutions that are still within the official borders of the Park: the Karnataka State Lawn Tennis Association, which had begun construction of a swimming pool within their premises in 2013; the Century Club, for beginning construction of a new residential block; and the Bangalore YMCA, located on Nrupathunga Road, for breaking ground for a multi-storeyed building on their premises. In all three cases, the court has issued stay orders, and construction has been stopped.

Not everyone is impressed with the CPWA's activities, however. The association, and its frontman, with their insistence that the Park is meant primarily for walkers, and that 'playing' and undefined 'illegal activities' are prosecutable offences, are seen by many other citizens' collectives doing their own bit for the Park as heavy-handed and autocratic. They are often accused of imposing a particular—and exclusionary—idea of how the Park as public commons should function.

Their disapproval does not bother Umesh. After all, he says, everything he does is only to protect and secure the Park, and he uses no other route to get there but the legal, constitutional one, which is also open to every other citizen to use. He believes implicitly that social media activism is for the birds—for change to happen, he argues, you need feet on the street, and that is something he is good at mobilizing. Also, whether he himself sees it that way or not, Umesh is a savvy branding strategist, who understands implicitly that people need a symbol or a totem to rally around, especially when the cause at hand is as abstract as a park.

The symbol he picked for CPWA and its campaign was an audacious one—it had been standing in plain sight in the Park for over a century, but very few Bangaloreans had even looked closely at it, let alone thought about co-opting it for their purposes. Its universal, unifying appeal

A pen-and-ink sketch from the 5 May, 1866, edition of the *Illustrated London News*, depicting the inauguration of the statue of Sir Mark Cubbon at Bangalore's Parade Ground.

Four years later, the statue moves to the front yard of the spanking new Attara Kacheri, where it stands for the next 150 years.

In 2020, Sir Mark is moved to his current spot inside Cubbon Park.

lay in the fact that no matter who or what you believed was part of the Park, there could be no argument about this one's fundamental right to be there. That symbol was the equestrian statue of Commissioner Mark Cubbon.

*

Right at its inception in 2012, the CPWA decided that it would henceforth observe the commissioner's birthday, 23rd August, as Mark Cubbon Day. At this time, Cubbon's statue stood where it had since the 1870s—in front of the Attara Kacheri. Around the statue, however, a lot had changed in the intervening years.

In 1952, Kengal Hanumanthaiah, who had been a member of the Indian Constituent Assembly, became the second Chief Minister of Karnataka. A fierce nationalist and staunch Mysorean, it riled him no end that his cabinet would have to work out of the Attara Kacheri, a structure that, to his mind, symbolized colonial power and Indian humiliation. His ire was only exacerbated when a group of Russian visitors he happened to be showing around the city asked him, in genuine puzzlement, 'Have you no architecture of your own? These are all European buildings.'

That did it. Without further ado, Hanumanthaiah sought permission to raze the Attara Kacheri to the ground. Permission was denied, so the new chief minister, laying aside the good sense that demanded that states stay austere in the early years after Independence, decided to raise a vast Dravidian-style building that was taller, broader, longer, and way, way grander than the colonial one, bang opposite the latter, with the specific intention of dwarfing it and rendering it insignificant. That building was the Vidhana Soudha.

When it was completed in 1956, the same year the States Reorganisation Act came into force, the Vidhana Soudha served as a powerful and magnificent symbol to unite the people of the newly carved-out state of Karnataka.

At some point after the state assembly and the cabinet had moved into the Vidhana Soudha in 1956, the back of the Attara Kacheri, which faced the Soudha, became its front entrance, perhaps because *noblesse oblige* demanded that the Raj relic never be allowed to avert its eyes from the magnificence of what had replaced it. Sir Mark himself was spared that humiliation—his back to the rancour that abounded behind him, he continued to gaze upon his Park from the Kacheri's original front entrance. As the trees around him grew taller and a fence with high gates came up around the High Court, Commissioner Cubbon faded from public memory.

Until, that is, the CPWA resurrected him. In the run-up to Mark Cubbon Day in 2013, the CPWA held a slew of press conferences to let the public know about the significance of the date and the man, even as they sought permission from the High Court to conduct a short ceremony, open to the public, on the day itself. But even with stringent security measures in place, the court was reluctant to have members of the public milling about its premises. Adding to the court's hesitation were protests and threats by Kannada activist and former MLA Vatal Nagaraj, who considered it deplorable that people were 'glorifying those who made Indians their slaves'. Way back in 1964, Vatal had successfully arm-twisted the government into demolishing an 18th-century British cenotaph*, so the court's concern was valid enough.

'If we do not want anything the British built, we will have to demolish the High Court building and Raj Bhavan

---

*The cenotaph commemorated the fall of the fort of Bengaluru in 1791, to the British army under Lord Cornwallis. It stood just outside the Halasuru Gate (or the eastern gate) of Kempegowda's original Bengaluru, and right outside the City Corporation Building, on a street then known as Cenotaph Road. Today, rechristened Nrupathunga Road, the cenotaph has been replaced by a statue of Kempegowda.

as well,' scoffs Umesh. 'As the Commissioner of Mysore, Cubbon's contribution to the development of Bangalore is undeniable. We should show some respect to people who contributed to our society.' With the support, overt and covert, of many Bangaloreans, Umesh eventually got the honourable court to see it his way.

At 7.30 a.m. on 23rd August 2013, Sir Mark's 238th birthday, the gates leading to the erstwhile front entrance of the Kacheri were quietly unlocked for the first time in decades. As the painted plaster lions snarled effetely from their perch at the bottom of the stairs, about twenty-five members of the CPWA gathered around the statue, against the backdrop of heavy police bandobast. It was Umesh, deservedly, who got to mount the ladder placed against the pedestal and place a freshly strung jasmine garland around the statue's neck. Sir Mark, one suspects, would have thoroughly appreciated this very Indian display of affection and respect.

Once the precedent had been set, there was no going back. Year after year, on Mark Cubbon Day, the CPWA re-enacted this little ceremony. But the rigmarole of getting permission and ID cards each time was hasslesome. In addition, a significant number of advocates and judges of the court were heartily sick of the annual circus. In 2019, High Court Judge Abhay Shreeniwas Oka passed an order for the statue to be moved out of the High Court premises and into the Park proper, so that the public could have unrestricted access to it. On 28 June 2020, with the assistance of the Karnataka Horticulture Department, Sir Mark moved to his new lodgings opposite the bandstand.

It was a triumph, of sorts, for the CPWA. While Umesh is delighted that his hero is now accessible to every citizen of the city, he is also aware that this eviction of Sir Mark from the High Court premises is another alarming sign of the Park's shrinking borders. 'If we citizens are not vigilant,' he says, 'that's all we'll one day have left of Cubbon Park—a statue and a tree.'

Epilogue

A Park for the Ages

Cubbon Park is part of the city's heritage, to be treasured and passed on from generation to generation. But one Cubbon Park cannot serve the expanding city—the effort should be to create more Cubbon Parks in newer precincts.

—Irfan Razack, Chairman and Managing Director of the Bangalore-based Prestige Group, one of India's leading developers of real estate

We should do nothing more in Cubbon Park. No more buildings, no more statues, no more trees. Sometimes we have to acknowledge that something is perfect and move on.

—Naresh Narasimhan, Principal Architect and Managing Partner at award-winning architecture firm Venkataramanan Associates

THE LAND ON WHICH CUBBON PARK LIES WAS SACRED TO Bangaloreans for at least a century before Richard Sankey clapped eyes on it. A saltwater tank called *Uppuneerina Kunte*, located close to the south-eastern boundary of the Park, has been central to the eleven-day festival of Karaga, a fixture on the city's annual calendar for over 250 years now. Dedicated to Draupadi, the feisty heroine of the Mahabharata, Karaga is essentially a festival that honours and celebrates water as Adi Shakti, the sacred feminine.

The Karaga procession through Kempegowda's original Bengaluru Pete on the ninth night of the festival draws huge crowds each year. The male priest, dressed in a sari and channelling Draupadi, is the cynosure of all eyes, as are the bare-chested, sword-wielding Veerakumaras who surround her, ready to defend her honour should the need arise. Both priest and warriors are drawn from the city's Tigala community, who consider themselves Draupadi's descendants.

It was the green-fingered Tigalas, experts at coaxing flowers and vegetables from the earth, who created Lalbagh at Hyder Ali's behest. It is not a stretch to believe that their descendants were also involved in the greening of Cubbon Park.

*

In February 2020, the Smart City Project for Bangalore held its first public consultation to present its Rs 40-crore

Cubbon Park Redevelopment Project. Part of the project involved repair and replacement jobs like redeveloping pathways, improving footpaths, marking cycling paths, mending gates and fences, replacing benches and dustbins, and desilting, recharging and connecting water bodies. Another part involved creating new spaces for specific groups and activities—a new 4-km jogging track, children's play zones, senior citizens' areas, yoga and meditation sections, a smog tower that would also include billboard space, covered picnic areas, more vegetable and fruit vending stalls, new signage, and an inclusive sensory park for the differently-abled.

It was the second part that shook up every community of citizens that cared about Cubbon Park. Discussions and debates erupted in the press, among urban planners and environmentalists, and across Park-loving citizens' organizations that didn't otherwise see eye to eye. The very idea that someone was considering adding so much 'unnecessary' cement, granite and neon to the Park, to ostensibly facilitate activities that the Park had already been lending itself to for years, sent tempers rising across the board. One by one, across a series of public consultations, petitions and signature campaigns through the first eighteen months of the COVID pandemic, Smart City was forced to drop several of its proposed additions to the Park.

'Most of Smart City's proposals went against every tenet of sustainability that I know of,' fumes entrepreneur

Sunita Kumar, who carried out one of the most sustained and vociferous protests against the Redevelopment Project. 'Why does a lung space like Cubbon Park need the illogicality of a humungous smog tower? Why does it need a giant granite obelisk as a signage board? Why should synthetic children's play areas be part of the Park when there is the entire 12.5-acre space of Bal Bhavan, meant specifically for children, adjacent to it? The Park is not a showcase for new design; anything that you put it has to be used, enjoyed, serve a purpose.'

Architects and consultants for the Smart City Project, on their part, denounce what they believe is an uninformed war waged purely on emotional grounds, meant simply to stymie any redevelopment, however necessary. 'The proposal was centred around preserving the Park's green cover and biodiversity,' said an architect who wished to remain anonymous. 'The interventions used only natural materials like stone and wood, and were designed to blend as seamlessly as possible into the Park's existing landscape. As a city changes, so should its public spaces, to accommodate the aspirations of a new generation of citizens. But some people simply cannot accommodate another point of view.'

Despite what this looks like, the truth is that the two adversaries are more alike than they imagine, at least as far as their concern for the Park goes. Sunita's connection with the Park is longstanding and deep—she has taken a walk there each morning for close to thirty years, and provided meals every day to over a hundred indies that live there, for at least a third of that time. For the architects, many of whom are themselves Bangalore-born and -raised, the opportunity to design interventions that would turn the Park into a role-model for sustainable, eco-friendly design is not just a dream project but a labour of love. 'We have wonderful childhood memories of Cubbon Park too,' says one. 'Why would we want to ruin it?'

In that face-off between the two sides, in the equal emotional ownership they both feel for the Park, and in their very different understanding of what it represents to the city, lies the key to Cubbon Park's enduring reign as Bangalore's most beloved green space. It is these—all the different claims its people have on it, all their expectations of it and all their aspirations for it—that keep the Park eternally contentious, relevant, and central to the Bangalorean heart and mind.

*

With the most recent threat to the Park having been averted, there is a sense of relief, but hardly any jubilation, among those responsible for the victory; everyone realizes that the respite is only temporary. The Park's own history, however, gives cause for hope. While the threats to the Park will be unrelenting, so will the courage of her Veerakumaras and Veerakumaris, who, like the flowers the Tigalas planted so lovingly all those years ago, will spring from the lush earth to protect her in each generation.

At some point in the Smart City wrangle, on the 'We ♥ Cubbon Park' WhatsApp group, a clearly frustrated member asked the question that was on everyone's minds: 'Why can't they just leave Cubbon Park alone?'

It is perhaps the Park's biggest tragedy, and greatest blessing, that Bangaloreans simply will not leave it alone.

My Cubbon Park

'Hyperlocal books,' said my friend and editor, Sudeshna Shome Ghosh, one fine Bangalore day (but aren't they all?) in the middle of the COVID pandemic. 'Not on cities, but on neighbourhoods. Would you like to do one? On a neighbourhood in Bangalore?'

My head nodded, eagerly. It's an involuntary thing it does—an affirmation, if you will, an approval, an acceptance—whenever Bangalore is mentioned. 'Which neighbourhood?' Sudeshna asked me.

I thought about it. It would have to be a part of the city I felt deeply about and knew well, not just in a head kind of way but in a heart-and-soul kind of way. It would have to be streets I had walked as a child and teen and adult, watching them change without really changing at all; for love would not be love if it altered when it alteration found. It would have to be some place that held my memories, and continued to hold me, in a fuzzy, comfortable, backdrop-to-my-life kind of way—no sharp edges, no jangling colours, no thunderous crescendos, no crashing diminuendos.

Malleswaram? School, junior college, my grandmother's

house, the smell of fresh-ground coffee and jasmine, the strains of Carnatic music—sure, but I seldom visited it now, ever since I had moved east, across Bangalore's great City-Cantonment divide. Kumara Park, where I grew up, and unfailingly distributed yellu-bella to a dozen neighbours each year, come Sankranthi? We-ell, that was just where I had lived, but life had always been elsewhere, like Malleswaram. Old Airport Road, my home for almost ten years? Duh. We're talking *neighbourhood*, bruh. The heart of the British Cantonment, then—MG Road, Brigade Road, Church Street—where, for close to a decade and a half, I had told stories of British barracks, beer and bacchanalia while leading history walks for the company I had co-founded, Bangalore Walks? I could rattle off dates and names and trivia about every hundred metres of those streets, but I had never lingered there too long; those spaces did not sing to me.

'I mean,' Sudeshna said, trying to help, 'it need not be a conventional neighbourhood. It could be a…'

'Park!' I shrieked. 'Cubbon Park!'

The violins began to play. Of *course!* Cubbon Park, purveyor of the popcorn-and-cotton-candy Sundays of my childhood, which welcomed me just as warmly when I returned home after a dozen years away in other cities and continents, this time with my children in tow, and then proceeded to win them over. Cubbon Park, glorious setting for the Century Club, which my dad was so chuffed to have finally gotten a membership to in his fiftieth year that he insisted on bearing us there each weekend in his ancient but beautifully kept Standard Herald, MYQ 6776 (although, it must be said, it was mum who usually drove). Cubbon Park, across the road from the over 100-year-old University Visvesvaraya College of Engineering that was my dad's alma mater, and mine. Cubbon Park, where I was successfully wooed, the now-husband keeping a wary eye out for marauding policemen who invariably threatened to drag us to lockup—or worse, call our parents. Cubbon Park, where I return at least twice every week, now that the children are grown and gone, with my dog-child, to the only open green space within city limits that welcomes her. Cubbon Park, always on the way to somewhere, offering me benedictions by the bushelful in every season—vast rain-tree canopies, just come into new leaf, shading whitehot April afternoons, wet flecks of gulmohur stippling my windshield in happy crimson as I drive through steel-grey June thunderstorms, clouds of pink tabebuia massed against the unbelievable blue of a crisp November sky...

Cubbon Park is not just a neighbourhood, I tell Sudeshna, it's a universe in and of itself, a consistently largehearted, always contested, uniquely Bangalorean ecosystem fashioned as much of trees and flowers and insects as of hearts and souls and minds.

Okay, she smiles, write about the Republic of Cubbon Park.

So I did.

Roopa Pai

Selected Bibliography

Colaco, Peter, *Bangalore: A Century of Tales from City and Cantonment*. Via Media Books, 2011.

De, Aditi, ed., *Multiple City: Writings on Bangalore*. Penguin, 2008.

Fernandes, Paul and Chicku Jayadeva, *Bangalore: Swinging in the Seventies*. Simova Education and Research Pvt. Ltd, 2014.

George, TJS, *Askew: A Short Biography of Bangalore*. Aleph Book Company, 2016.

Ismail, Sir Mirza, *My Public Life*. George Allen & Unwin Ltd, 1954.

Issar, TP, *The City Beautiful*. Bangalore Urban Arts Commission, 1998.

Iyer, Meera, *Discovering Bengaluru*. INTACH Bengaluru, 2019.

Lang, Major AM, ed., *Professional Papers on Indian Engineering, Vol II*. 1873.

Mathur, Anuradha and Dilip da Cunha, *Deccan Traverses: The Making of Bangalore's Terrain*. Rupa, 2006.

Nair, Janaki, *The Promise of the Metropolis: Bangalore's Twentieth Century*. Oxford University Press, 2005.

Pani, Narendar, Sindhu Radhakrishna and Kishor G. Bhat, eds, *Bengaluru, Bangalore, Bengaluru: Imaginations and Their Times*. Sage Publications, 2008.

Russell, William Howard, *The Prince of Wales' Tour of India—A Diary in India*. 1877.

Sastri, KN Venkatasubba, *The Administration of Mysore under Sir Mark Cubbon*. 1932.

Siddalingaiah, *A Word with You, World: The Autobiography of a Poet*, translated by SR Ramakrishna. Navayana, 2013.

Srinivas, Smriti, *Landscapes of Urban Memory: The Sacred and the Civic in India's Hi-tech City*. Orient Longman, 2004.

Thiruvady, VR, *Lalbagh: Sultan's Garden to Public Park*. Bangalore Environment Trust, 2020.

Thornton, Thomas Henry, *General Sir Richard Meade and the Feudatory States of Central and Southern India*. 1898.

Vibart, Colonel HM, *Addiscombe: Its Heroes and Men of Note*. 1894.

Wilks, Colonel Mark, *History of Mysore*. 1810. Edited by Murray Hammick, Asian Educational Services, 1989.